Mental Toughness For Young Athletes:

The Ultimate Parent's Guide to Fuel Your Child's Competitive Sport with 10 Strategies and 5-Minute Mindset Drills

Micheal and Megan Alexi

liable for any hardship or damages that may befall them after undertaking information described herein.

Additionally, the information in the following pages is intended only for informational purposes and should thus be thought of as universal. As befitting its nature, it is presented without assurance regarding its prolonged validity or interim quality. Trademarks that are mentioned are done without written consent and can in no way be considered an endorsement from the trademark holder.

Table of Content

Introduction

Greetings to all the dedicated parents out there, those who proudly wear the titles of mentors, cheerleaders, and advocates for their young athletes.

I am Michael Alexi, and I stand before you not just as an author but as someone who shares your passion for nurturing the potential in our young sports enthusiasts.

As a parent myself and a director of a Californian soccer team, my journey in the world of youth sports has been a dynamic blend of exhilarating victories and valuable lessons learned.

But, I've been on this transformative adventure with my own daughter, Megan.

In the pulsating heart of competitive sports, it's not just physical prowess that separates champions from the rest; it's mental toughness. Mental toughness isn't just about winning trophies; it's about nurturing young minds to embrace challenges as opportunities for growth. It's about shaping athletes who not only excel in their chosen sports but also thrive in life, equipped with skills like discipline, leadership, and stress management that transcend the boundaries of the playing field.

Our young athletes are not just future sports stars; they are the leaders, problem solvers, and change-makers of tomorrow. It is our duty, as parents and mentors, to provide them with the mental fortitude they need to succeed in every aspect of life. Through the chapters ahead, we will delve deep into the intricacies of building mental toughness in young athletes. We will explore the crucial role parents play in this process, offering insights on involvement, emotional support, and effective communication. We'll unlock the potential of the subconscious mind and delve into the power of visualization as a mental training tool. We'll guide you in setting and achieving effective goals and teach you how to draw inspiration from the pros.

Meditation will become a valuable tool in your toolkit as we explore its benefits for young athletes. We'll also introduce the concept of *"playing small"* and the art of reducing performance pressure. You'll discover the significance of practicing slower, not just on the field but in life, and how it can lead to improved performance. Together, we'll explore strategies for intensive training and overcoming challenges with a warrior mentality.

Our journey wouldn't be complete without emphasizing the importance of recovery and mental cooldown techniques. We'll guide you on how to instill post-training relaxation routines into your athlete's life for optimal well-being.

As we journey through these pages, keep in mind that this book isn't just a manual; it's a conversation, a partnership. It's an opportunity for you to empower your young athletes, to help them rise above challenges, and to witness their growth, both on and off the field.

Throughout this book, we will offer practical exercises, real-life examples, and actionable steps to guide you. But remember, every young athlete is unique, and the path to success may take unexpected turns. We invite you to embrace this journey with an open heart and an open mind, ready to adapt and support your child's individual growth.

My personal journey

I'm Michael Alexi, a dedicated soccer team manager in California. I've spent years working alongside passionate coaches and talented athletes, gaining valuable insights into the world of sports psychology.

Allow me to share my own personal journey in the world of youth sports.

At the heart of my journey is my 16-year-old daughter, Megan. Megan has been immersed in the world of soccer since she was just 4 years old. Today, she stands proudly as a forward on a remarkable Californian soccer team, actively participating in competitive tournaments. Her dream? To one day represent the national women's soccer team. Megan's unwavering dedication to her sport has not only fueled her ambitions but also served as a constant source of inspiration for me.

In my quest to support Megan's athletic passion and contribute meaningfully to my profession, I embarked on a transformative inner-growth journey. I enrolled in a specialized program known as **"Unleash Your Mental Strength,"** tailored to the world of sports. This program provided me with invaluable insights into the profound impact of mental toughness on athletic performance.

As I delved deeper into this journey, I became part of a community of like-minded parents who were also navigating the intricate landscape of youth sports. Together, we embarked on group coaching sessions, sharing our experiences and insights. I had the privilege of listening to both parents and young athletes, understanding their challenges and triumphs, and gaining a holistic perspective on the critical role parents play in their children's athletic development.

With the consent of these fellow parents and their young athletes, I compiled a treasure trove of experiences and stories. These stories, gathered from those who had undertaken a similar path, not only enriched my understanding but also inspired me to take action. My goal was twofold: first, to impart the valuable knowledge gained from this journey to my daughter, Megan, and second, to create a comprehensive guide for parents of young athletes and aspiring sports stars.

The culmination of this endeavor is what you now hold in your hands—a guidebook designed to empower parents with the tools and insights needed to guide their young athletes through the labyrinth of self-confidence issues and performance anxiety. It's a testament to the collective wisdom of dedicated parents and the unwavering determination of young athletes, like Megan, who inspire us all to strive for excellence both on and off the field.

This book represents the fusion of personal experiences, professional expertise, and a passionate commitment to nurturing the next generation of athletes. Let's go out on this adventure together to develop your child athlete's mental toughness and unwavering confidence so they can reach new heights.

Chapter 1: The Role of Parents in Building Mental Toughness

As parents, we share a common dream for our children - to see them flourish and succeed in every aspect of life. For many of us, this dream extends to the realm of youth sports, where we hope to witness our children not only excel physically but also grow mentally strong. We understand that sports have the potential to instill essential life skills such as discipline, resilience, leadership, and stress management. However, the path to achieving both physical and mental excellence can be filled with challenges, and that's where our role as parents becomes paramount.

In this chapter, we embark on a journey to explore the pivotal role parents play in building the mental toughness of young athletes. We will delve into the intricate dynamics of parent-child relationships within the context of youth sports, emphasizing the importance of effective communication, emotional support, and fostering trust. Our aim is to provide practical, easy-to-understand guidance to help parents guide their young athletes through the development of mental toughness, particularly when their children grapple with issues like in-game self-confidence and performance anxiety. We firmly believe that by respecting our children's character and personality while setting and achieving goals together, we can empower them to thrive both on and off the field.

We live in a world where competition begins at an increasingly young age, and the pressure to perform can be overwhelming for our children. While physical skills are undoubtedly essential, it's often the mental fortitude that distinguishes champions from contenders.

Being mentally strong doesn't mean being unbending or stoic; rather, it means learning how to tackle obstacles head-on, get past failures, and keep a positive outlook when things become rough. Resilience, self-assurance, and efficient stress and anxiety management are all included.

As parents, we recognize that nurturing these qualities in our young athletes can have a transformative impact on their sports journey and, by extension, their lives.

When our children face self-confidence issues or performance anxiety during games, it's easy to feel helpless or unsure of how to support them effectively. This is precisely where our journey begins. Together, we will explore strategies to help parents understand and address these challenges, fostering mental toughness in their young athletes. We will emphasize the importance of building strong parent-child relationships based on trust, open communication, and empathy, as these are the cornerstones of guiding our children toward success in sports and beyond.

Involvement of Parents in the Mental Development of Young Athletes

The Inspiring Story of the Williams Family

Understanding the vital role of parental involvement in the mental development of young athletes requires delving into real-life examples that showcase the power of nurturing a strong and resilient mindset in sports. In this narrative, we'll explore the remarkable journey of the Williams family and their son, Alex, as they navigate the challenging world of youth basketball.

John and Sarah Williams, residents of a quiet suburban town in the heart of Chicago, have always been passionate about sports. As former athletes themselves, they understood the life lessons and personal growth that could be derived from participation in sports. When their son, Alex, expressed a keen interest in basketball from a young age, they embraced his passion with open arms.

Alex, a bright and determined young boy, exhibited an exceptional aptitude for basketball early on. His parents, John and Sarah, recognized his potential and believed that his journey in the world of sports could be a remarkable avenue for personal development. With their support, Michael began his journey towards becoming not just a talented athlete but also a resilient and well-rounded individual.

John, a former amateur basketball player who had once nurtured dreams of playing professionally, took on the role of Alex's primary mentor and coach. His experience in the sport allowed him to teach Alex the technical aspects of basketball while instilling essential life skills.

John's approach was marked by an emphasis on discipline, unwavering determination, and resilience. He shared stories from his own youth basketball days, recounting both the triumphs and tribulations he had encountered. He made it clear to Alex that success in basketball, as in life, was not solely defined by victories but by the ability to bounce back from failures.

One of the key lessons John imparted was the importance of setting realistic goals and working diligently towards them. He encouraged Alex to establish both short-term and long-term goals, which ranged from improving his batting average to developing leadership skills on the field.

Sarah, a dedicated healthcare professional, brought her unique qualities to the family's dynamic. She possessed an innate capacity for empathy and emotional support, which she channeled into nurturing Alex's emotional well-being.

In moments of frustration or disappointment, which are inevitable in the world of sports, Sarah played the role of a compassionate and understanding confidante. She taught Alex that it was natural to experience a range of emotions but emphasized the importance of processing these feelings constructively.

Sarah encouraged open communication within the family, ensuring that Alex felt comfortable expressing his thoughts, doubts, and anxieties. This not only strengthened the parent-child bond but also allowed for a holistic understanding of Alex's emotional landscape.

One of the cornerstones of the Williams family's approach to Alex's development was their commitment to open and insightful family discussions. These conversations often revolved around detailed game reviews, performance analyses, and the formulation of strategies for future matches.

In these discussions, Alex's voice was valued, and his opinions were heard. He was an active participant in setting his own athletic and personal goals, which created a sense of accountability. The family's collective effort in planning and strategizing made Alex feel that he had a team both on and off the field.

One of the most profound challenges Alex faced occurred during a crucial regional tournament. In this high-pressure event, he made critical errors on the field and struggled at bat, contributing to the team's unexpected defeat. It was a defining moment that tested his resilience and mental toughness.

Instead of reproaching their son or placing undue pressure on him, John and Sarah stood firmly by his side. They turned this experience into a valuable lesson on how to handle adversity. They shared stories of professional athletes who had weathered turbulent periods in their careers but ultimately emerged stronger and more determined.

This experience instilled in Alex the understanding that defeats were not indicators of failure but opportunities for growth. It taught him that the ability to bounce back from setbacks was an essential aspect of mental toughness.

The Williams family's story is a poignant testament to the pivotal role of parental involvement in the mental development of young athletes. John and Sarah Williams did not merely attend their son's games; they actively participated in his growth as an athlete and, more importantly, as a resilient and determined individual.

Their story exemplifies that effective parental involvement transcends the technicalities of sports. The Williams family's journey underscores the profound impact parents can have on their children's development as athletes and as well-rounded individuals. Through mentorship, empathetic communication, and the ability to transform defeats into opportunities for growth, parents like John and Sarah Williams play a pivotal role in shaping the future of young athletes. Their legacy is a reminder that sports can be a vehicle not only for athletic success but also for personal growth and resilience.

Emotional and Motivational Support: Nurturing Young Athletes' Mental Toughness

This chapter delves deep into the crucial aspects of emotional and motivational support that parents can provide to foster their child's mental toughness. We will explore the profound impact of a positive support system on young athletes' development and how it can help them overcome challenges, build resilience, and ultimately excel in their chosen sports. Emotional support is the cornerstone of a young athlete's mental well-being. It involves creating an environment where children feel safe, understood, and valued, regardless of their performance on the field. Parents must recognize that the pressure to succeed in competitive sports can take a toll on their child's emotional health. Therefore, providing a nurturing and empathetic atmosphere is paramount.

A Real-Life Example: The Johnson Family
Consider the Johnson family as an illustrative example. Mark Johnson, a successful attorney, and his wife, Diana, both former collegiate athletes, have a 14-year-old daughter, Emma, who is a budding gymnast with aspirations of making it to the national level. Despite their demanding careers, Mark and Diana prioritize creating an emotionally supportive environment for Emma. They regularly engage in open

conversations with her about the challenges she faces in her sport and actively listen to her concerns. By doing so, they have fostered trust and communication, allowing Emma to express her fears and anxieties without the fear of judgment. When Emma encountered a period of self-doubt after a series of disappointing performances, her parents' unwavering emotional support played a crucial role. They reassured her that their love and support were not contingent on her success in gymnastics. This foundation of emotional security empowered Emma to regain her confidence and motivation. With her parents as pillars of support, she embraced her training with renewed vigor, eventually earning a spot on the state gymnastics team.

Motivation is the driving force behind a young athlete's commitment to their sport. Parents can contribute significantly to their child's motivation by understanding their individual needs and aspirations. Motivational support involves helping children set goals, stay focused, and persevere through challenges.

A Real-Life Example: The Patel Family
The Patel family provides an inspiring example of effective motivational support. Aiden Patel, a talented 16-year-old tennis player, dreams of playing at the collegiate level. His parents, Priya and Raj, recognized Aiden's passion for the sport from a young age and made it a point to align their

support with his aspirations. They involved him in setting realistic yet challenging goals, encouraging him to take ownership of his tennis journey.

When Aiden faced a string of losses in a particularly competitive season, his motivation began to waver. However, his parents were quick to remind him of his long-term goals and the progress he had made. They emphasized that setbacks were a natural part of any athlete's journey and an opportunity for growth. Through their unwavering motivational support, Priya and Raj helped Aiden develop the resilience needed to bounce back stronger. He went on to secure a scholarship to a Division I university, fulfilling his dream.

Strategies for Effective Emotional and Motivational Support

While emotional and motivational support is crucial, it's essential for parents to strike a balance between nurturing their child's passion and not overwhelming them with expectations. Here are some strategies for parents to provide effective support:

Active listening: Take the time to listen to your child's thoughts, feelings, and concerns related to their sport. Create a safe space where they can express themselves without fear of criticism.

Empathy and Validation: Validate your child's emotions, even if they seem irrational or disproportionate. Empathizing with their struggles fosters trust and connection.

Set realistic expectations: Encourage goal-setting but ensure the goals are achievable and aligned with your child's abilities and ambitions. Unrealistic expectations can lead to stress and burnout.

Celebrate effort, not just outcomes: Praise your child's hard work, dedication, and perseverance, irrespective of the competition's outcome. This reinforces the importance of the process rather than just results.

Provide autonomy: Involve your child in decision-making related to their sport, such as setting training schedules and choosing competitions. This empowers them and nurtures their intrinsic motivation.

Seek professional guidance: If you're unsure about how to best support your young athlete's emotional and motivational needs, consider consulting with a sports psychologist or counselor who specializes in youth sports.

In conclusion, the emotional and motivational support parents provide can be the bedrock of a young athlete's mental toughness. By creating a nurturing environment, setting realistic goals, and fostering passion and resilience, parents can empower their children to thrive in their sports journey. In the following chapters, we will continue to explore how parents can play an active role in enhancing their young athlete's mental toughness and overall development.

Building trust and understanding: The Smiths have always been a shining example of how effective communication between parents and young athletes can make a significant difference in a child's sports journey.

John and Brooke Smith are proud parents of two athletic children, Alison and Ethan, who have been actively participating in various sports since a young age. Their commitment to nurturing their children's sports passion while maintaining a balanced and supportive family environment has truly set them apart.

John, a lawyer, and Brooke, a nurse, understand the importance of open and honest communication. They believe that fostering a strong parent-child relationship through effective communication is just as crucial as practicing free throws or perfecting a backhand swing. From the early days of T-ball to the intense competition of high school soccer and tennis, the Smiths have always been there for their children. One particular instance that highlights their commitment to communication happened during Alison's freshman year of high school. Alison, an aspiring tennis player, faced a challenging situation when she began to struggle with her serves. Rather than pushing her harder or criticizing her performance, John and Brooke decided to sit down with her and initiate a conversation. They asked open-ended questions and actively listened to her concerns. Brooke revealed that she was feeling anxious about her serves and feared letting her team down during important matches.

Through this heartfelt conversation, John and Brooke not only provided emotional support to Alison but also reassured her that mistakes and setbacks are part of every athlete's journey. They encouraged her to share her feelings and doubts openly, creating a safe space for her to express herself without judgment. This conversation not only improved Alison's mental state but also strengthened the bond between parents and child.

The Andersons, another sports-loving family, have also mastered the art of effective communication in the world of youth athletics. David and Lisa Anderson are both educators, which gives them valuable insights into the dynamics of learning and personal growth. Their children, Lily and Noah, have been actively involved in competitive swimming for years.

One memorable instance of their effective communication occurred when Noah, an aspiring swimmer with dreams of competing at the collegiate level, faced a challenging plateau in his performance. Instead of focusing solely on his times and rankings, the Andersons took a different approach. They held a family meeting where they discussed Noah's goals, dreams, and any obstacles he was facing.

Noah expressed his concerns about the rigorous training schedule and the pressure to perform well academically. David and Lisa, drawing from their educational background, worked collaboratively with their son to create a manageable timetable that balanced his swimming commitments and schoolwork effectively. This not only eased Noah's stress but also empowered him to take ownership of his schedule and goals.

Lastly, let's delve into the Wilsons' story, where effective communication played a pivotal role in their children's sports journey. Mark and Emily Wilson, both engineers, have three children, Mia, Jackson, and Olivia, who are passionate about soccer. Their family is a testament to how open dialogue can lead to holistic development in young athletes.

During one soccer season, Jackson, the middle child, was struggling with a lack of motivation. His performance on the field had dipped, and his enthusiasm seemed to wane. Concerned but supportive, Mark and Emily decided to take Jackson out for ice cream and engage in a candid conversation. They encouraged him to share his feelings and thoughts about soccer.

Jackson admitted that he was feeling overwhelmed by the pressure to excel, not only from his coaches and teammates but also from himself. Mark and Emily assured him that they loved and supported him, regardless of his performance. They emphasized that his happiness and well-being were the top priorities. This conversation relieved the burden of unrealistic expectations from Jackson's shoulders, allowing him to rediscover his love for the sport.

Effective communication between parents and young athletes involves not just verbal communication but also non-verbal clues. Body language, gestures, and facial expressions are examples of nonverbal communication.

For the Smiths, Andersons, and Wilsons, their non-verbal cues consistently conveyed empathy, support, and understanding during crucial conversations with their children. A comforting hug, a reassuring smile, or a comforting touch can often speak louder than words and help young athletes feel valued and secure.

These three families—The Smiths, The Andersons, and The Wilsons—show us that effective communication is a cornerstone of building trust and understanding in the world of youth sports. While their backgrounds and stories differ, the common thread of open and empathetic communication runs through each of them. In the next section, we'll look at doable tactics that parents can use to improve their communication abilities and foster healthy relationships with their young athletes.

In conclusion, as we wrap up our exploration of the vital role parents play in building mental toughness for young athletes, it's essential to reflect on the transformative power of effective communication, emotional support, and goal-setting. Throughout this chapter, we've delved into the lives of three remarkable families—the Smiths, the Andersons, and the Wilsons—each demonstrating a unique approach to parenting in the realm of youth sports.

We've learned from the Smiths how open and honest communication, coupled with unwavering emotional support, can help a young athlete like Emma overcome performance anxiety and regain her self-confidence. The Andersons have shown us the significance of setting realistic goals and striking a balance between athletic pursuits and academic responsibilities. Finally, the Wilsons' story has emphasized the value of addressing personal doubts and fears through heart-to-heart conversations, paving the way for a resilient mindset.

But what ties these narratives together is the unwavering commitment of parents who understand that fostering mental toughness in their children goes beyond the scoreboard. It's about nurturing individuals who are not only adept at their chosen sports but also equipped with life skills such as resilience, discipline, and effective communication.

As parents, it's crucial to remember that our children are not clones but **unique individuals** with distinct character traits, strengths, and areas for growth. The journey toward mental toughness may look different for each young athlete, and that's perfectly fine. What matters is our unwavering support, our willingness to listen, and our commitment to being their biggest champions.

Parents, you have now been armed with insights, strategies, and practical advice on how to navigate the challenges and opportunities that youth sports present. Remember that the path to building mental toughness is a continuous one, marked by successes and setbacks, moments of elation, and times of introspection. Always keep the lines of communication open, cherish the small victories, and offer a secure environment where they can talk about their hopes and uncertainties.

Embrace the idea that setbacks are opportunities for growth, and through every challenge they face, they have the chance to emerge stronger and more resilient.

In the chapters to come, we will continue to explore various facets of mental toughness, from visualization techniques to goal mastery and strategies for competition days. These insights will further equip you to guide your young athletes toward becoming the best versions of themselves, both in sports and in life.

With determination, empathy, and unwavering support, you can be the driving force behind your child's journey toward mental toughness, self-confidence, and ultimate success. This is not just about becoming champions on the field; it's about raising remarkable individuals who are poised to excel in every aspect of life.

Chapter 2: Strengthening Your Young Athlete's Subconscious Mind

Welcome to the heart of our journey, in this chapter, we delve into the intricate realm of your young athlete's subconscious mind and the profound influence it exerts on their athletic performance. We will provide you, as parents, with practical, easy-to-understand guidance on not only harnessing the power of a positive mindset but also emphasizing the importance of aligning inner thoughts with desires.

As you navigate through this chapter, envision the transformative impact you can have on your child's life. Picture them confidently stepping onto the field, court, or track, not only armed with physical prowess but also equipped with a deep understanding of how their internal dialogue influences their external performance.

Before we dive into the practical strategies, it's essential to grasp the significance of the subconscious mind and its role in molding your young athlete's performance. This hidden facet of the mind holds sway over thoughts, emotions, and behaviors, often operating beneath the surface of conscious awareness. In the context of sports, it becomes the silent orchestrator of your child's responses to the challenges they face on the field.

Imagine your young athlete, standing at a pivotal moment in a game, with the subconscious mind coming into play. In this high-pressure scenario, their inner dialogue can either empower them with unwavering confidence or undermine their performance with self-doubt and anxiety.

Now, envision a different scenario where your child's subconscious mind is fortified with positivity and resilience. They confront the same high-pressure situation with self-assuredness, ready to give their best. It's the same talent, the same skills, but with an entirely different outcome.

This is the power of the subconscious mind. It can either propel your child to new heights or shackle them with limitations. As parents, it's your role to nurture and guide this hidden aspect of their mental game.

One crucial aspect of strengthening the subconscious mind is cultivating an inner dialogue that aligns with your child's desires and goals. This internal communication shapes their self-belief, confidence, and ability to navigate adversity effectively.

Consider the importance of your young athlete's thoughts echoing their aspirations. When their inner dialogue is aligned with their desires, they are more likely to manifest their goals with conviction. It's about teaching your child to be not only the captain of their body but also the master of their mind. In the upcoming chapters, we will delve into exercises and strategies designed to help your child cultivate mental toughness gradually.

These exercises will empower them to reframe negative self-talk, embrace positive affirmations, and establish harmony between their inner thoughts and their desires.

As parents, you play a strong role in fostering this alignment. Your guidance, support, and understanding are instrumental in helping your child build a strong foundation of mental toughness. Together, you will embark on a journey that not only enhances their athletic performance but also equips them with invaluable life skills

The subconscious mind and its impact on athletic performance

Deep within the intricate landscape of the human mind, lies a treasure trove of experiences, emotions, and beliefs that silently shape our thoughts, actions, and ultimately, our athletic performance. This enigmatic realm is none other than the subconscious mind. To truly grasp the profound impact of the subconscious on an athlete's journey, it's imperative to delve deeper into its workings and understand when and how it begins to influence individuals in the realm of sports. Understanding the Subconscious Mind is crucial: the subconscious mind is the vast reservoir of thoughts, memories, and impressions that accumulate throughout a person's life, primarily during their formative years. This hidden realm operates beneath the surface of conscious awareness, making it elusive yet incredibly potent. It's a repository where every life experience, from early childhood memories to recent events, is stored, cataloged, and processed. For athletes, the subconscious mind serves as both a confidant and a formidable adversary. It subtly molds self-perception, motivation, focus, and responses to stress and pressure. It shapes the athlete's inner dialogue during critical moments of competition, and it's the source of both self-doubt and self-belief.

In essence, it acts as the quiet architect of an athlete's performance, largely unbeknownst to the athlete themselves.

The formation and development of the subconscious mind are ongoing processes that begin at birth and continue throughout one's life. However, it is during a child's early years that this realm of the mind is most impressionable and susceptible to external influences.

Here's a closer look at how the subconscious mind evolves in young athletes I learned during my course "Unleash Your Mental Strength".

Infancy to Early Childhood (0-7 years): This phase is characterized by the rapid absorption of information and experiences. During these formative years, the subconscious mind acts as a sponge, soaking up everything from a child's environment, including family dynamics, early social interactions, and emotional experiences. These early imprints lay the foundation for self-esteem, self-worth, and beliefs about one's capabilities, which can significantly influence an athlete's performance later in life.

Middle Childhood to Adolescence (7-17 years): As children grow, their subconscious mind continues to evolve.

This period is marked by increased social interactions, academic challenges, and, importantly, involvement in sports. The beliefs and attitudes formed during these years regarding competition, teamwork, and personal abilities become integral components of the athlete's subconscious. Coaches, parents, peers, and personal experiences all contribute to shaping the athlete's self-concept and their perception of their athletic potential.

It's important to note that while the subconscious mind undergoes significant development during these early years, its plasticity persists throughout life. This means that individuals can continue to influence and reprogram their subconscious beliefs and patterns, even in adulthood.

The subconscious mind of young athletes is not developed in isolation. It is continually shaped and molded by various external influences, including parental, coaches and fellows influence.

Parents play an important role in a young athlete's subconscious development. Their words, actions, and attitudes significantly impact how a child perceives themselves and their athletic abilities. Positive reinforcement, encouragement, and constructive feedback can contribute to a healthy self-image, while excessive pressure, criticism, or unrealistic expectations can introduce self-doubt and anxiety.

Coaches serve as mentors who can either nurture an athlete's self-belief or undermine it. The guidance, feedback, and mentoring provided by coaches can leave a lasting impression on an athlete's subconscious. Effective coaching techniques, which include building confidence, setting achievable goals, and emphasizing effort rather than just outcomes, can positively shape an athlete's mental landscape.

Peer interactions and team dynamics also influence the subconscious mind of young athletes. Supportive teammates and a positive team culture can reinforce an athlete's self-confidence and motivation. Conversely, a negative or competitive team environment may introduce stress and self-doubt.

Successes and failures in sports competitions are significant influencers of the subconscious mind.
Repeated successes can bolster an athlete's self-belief, while failures can introduce doubts and fears. How these experiences are processed, and the narratives that athletes construct around them, further shape their subconscious beliefs.

In the chapters that follow, we will explore practical strategies and exercises designed to tap into the potential of the subconscious mind in young athletes. These techniques aim to empower parents, coaches, and athletes themselves to positively influence the subconscious, fostering mental toughness that extends beyond the realm of sports and into the broader canvas of life. We're going to go on an adventure together to fortify and master the subconscious mind., equipping young athletes with the mental fortitude needed to excel in their chosen sports and beyond.

Exercises to Strengthen the Subconscious Mind: Harnessing the Power of Positive Affirmations

In the pursuit of enhancing mental toughness and athletic performance in young athletes, this chapter focuses on practical exercises aimed at fortifying the subconscious mind through the use of **positive affirmations**.

Positive affirmations are an invaluable tool used by athletes of all levels to reprogram their subconscious minds, thereby cultivating constructive self-beliefs and attitudes that can significantly influence performance.

Positive affirmations are concise and optimistic statements designed to challenge and counteract negative thoughts or beliefs. They serve as potent instruments for reprogramming the subconscious mind, fostering constructive self-beliefs and attitudes that directly impact an athlete's performance. Athletes, both aspiring and accomplished, have long recognized the transformative potential of positive affirmations. They understand that athletic prowess is not solely determined by physical abilities but is profoundly influenced by the mindset and beliefs held within the deepest recesses of the subconscious.

The Legacy of Michael Jordan: A Case Study

Few athletes have harnessed the power of positive affirmations as effectively as the basketball legend Michael Jordan. Jordan's affirmation, *"I can accept failure; everyone fails at something. But I can't accept not trying,"* exemplifies his unwavering self-belief and determination. This affirmation not only fueled his relentless work ethic but also helped him bounce back from failures and setbacks.

Jordan's extraordinary success was not solely attributable to his physical gifts but was equally shaped by his mental fortitude. His belief in himself and his ability to persevere through adversity set him apart as one of the greatest athletes of all time.

The practical application consists in crafting effective affirmations.

Parents, coaches, and young athletes can collaborate to create tailored affirmations that align with specific goals and challenges.

The following principles that I use to help my daughter Megan to establish her daily affirmations can guide you for their construction and effective use:

Personalization: Affirmations should be personalized to resonate with the athlete's unique journey, goals, and areas of focus. They should reflect the individual's aspirations and desires.

Present Tense: Effective affirmations are framed in the present tense, as if the desired outcome is already a reality. For example, *"I am a resilient and confident athlete."*

Positivity: Affirmations should emphasize positive attributes, behaviors, and outcomes. The goal is to cultivate a positive self-concept and self-worth.

Specificity: While affirmations should be positive and concise, they can also be specific. For instance, an athlete aspiring to improve their free throw shooting might use the affirmation, *"I am calm and focused when shooting free throws."*

Believability: Athletes should genuinely believe in the affirmations they recite. If an affirmation feels unrealistic or unattainable, it may be less effective.

The most decorated Olympian of all time, swimmer Michael Phelps, utilized positive affirmations to overcome challenges and setbacks throughout his career. When he encountered difficulties, Phelps often repeated affirmations like *"It's okay to struggle"* and *"I can overcome anything"* to refocus his mindset and maintain his mental edge.

Phelps understood that the power of affirmations extended beyond the pool and into all aspects of his life. By maintaining a positive and resilient mindset, he was not only able to achieve unprecedented success in the water but also to overcome personal obstacles.

Let's explore affirmations used by other prominent athletes, each offering a unique perspective on the potential of positive self-talk:

Serena Williams: Tennis legend Serena Williams is well-known for her affirmations, which include *"I am strong," "I am powerful,"* and *"I am the best."* These statements reinforce her self-belief and resilience during matches, serving as a source of motivation and mental strength.

Carli Lloyd: The renowned soccer player Carli Lloyd employs situational affirmations to stay focused and confident during high-pressure penalty shootouts. Her affirmation, *"I've got this,"* reinforces her self-belief and helps her execute with precision when the stakes are high.

Usain Bolt: Sprinting legend Usain Bolt famously used affirmations like *"I am a champion"* and *"I can achieve anything"* to pursue his goal of becoming the fastest man on Earth. These affirmations fueled his relentless pursuit of excellence and played a central role in his record-breaking achievements.

Michael Jordan: As previously mentioned, Michael Jordan's affirmation, *"I can accept failure; everyone fails at something. But I can't accept not trying,"* exemplifies his unwavering self-belief and determination. This affirmation helped him bounce back from failures and setbacks on his path to greatness.

Incorporating these real-life examples into discussions with young athletes can inspire them to embrace positive affirmations as a tool for personal growth and enhanced performance. By witnessing the successes of these iconic athletes, young athletes can appreciate the impact of a resilient and positive mindset.

Daily practice and consistency is a success strategy. The efficacy of positive affirmations hinges on their consistent repetition. Athletes should integrate affirmations into their daily routines, ideally in the morning, before training or competition, and before bedtime. Repetition allows the subconscious mind to gradually internalize and embrace the affirmations, leading to a shift in beliefs and attitudes.

Positive affirmations are particularly valuable in fostering resilience—the ability to bounce back from setbacks and remain undeterred by challenges. They instill the belief that setbacks are temporary and that progress is always possible.

In conclusion, positive affirmations are a dynamic and accessible tool that can profoundly impact an athlete's journey. When practiced with intention and consistency, they have the power to reshape the subconscious mind, bolster self-belief, enhance resilience, and lay the foundation for athletic greatness.

Harnessing the Power of Positive Mindset in 5 Minute

In the realm of competitive sports, a young athlete's mental strength can be the difference between victory and defeat. This chapter is dedicated to short yet highly effective mindset exercises, specifically created for players in the 8–18 age range.

By dedicating just five minute to these exercises, your child can develop resilience, self-belief, and emotional well-being. I use to do these exercises with my daughter Megan every day!"

Exercise 1: Power of Positive Affirmations (2 Minute)

Positive affirmations are a cornerstone of mental strength. They are short, impactful statements designed to foster self-confidence and self-belief. Encourage your young athlete to create a list of personal affirmations tailored to their goals and aspirations. Here are some examples:

- *"I am strong, capable, and resilient."*
- *"I embrace challenges and grow from them."*
- *"I am a valuable asset to my team."*
- *"I have the skills and determination to succeed."*

Have your child repeat these affirmations daily, ideally in the morning and before any sports-related activities. This practice helps in boosting self-esteem and maintaining a positive mindset.

Real-Life Inspiration: Consider the legendary basketball player Michael Jordan. He was renowned for his unwavering self-belief, often repeating affirmations such as, "*I can accept failure; everyone fails at something. But I can't accept not trying.*"

Exercise 2: Breathing for Calmness (1 Minute)
Deep breathing techniques are essential for managing anxiety and maintaining focus during high-pressure sports situations. Spend a minute with your child practicing deep diaphragmatic breathing. Breathe in deeply through your nose, letting your abdomen expand, and then softly release the breath through your mouth. Deep breaths like these can be a lifesaver during tense moments in competitions.

Real-Life Inspiration: Olympic swimmer Michael Phelps relied on controlled breathing techniques to stay calm and focused during races. He understood the value of composure in high-stakes situations.

Exercise 3: Gratitude and Success Journal (2 Minute)

Gratitude is a potent tool for cultivating a positive outlook. Encourage your young athlete to maintain a gratitude and success journal. Each day, have them write down at least one thing they're grateful for and one situation where they successfully handled a problem or challenge. This exercise fosters positivity and resilience

- *"Today, I'm grateful for the support of my teammates."*
- *"I successfully managed my pre-competition nerves today."*
- *"I'm thankful for the opportunity to play the sport I love."*

Real-Life Inspiration: Tennis sensation Serena Williams is known for keeping a gratitude journal to maintain a positive mindset, even during challenging matches. She often expresses gratitude for her family's support and her love for the sport.

By dedicating just five minute a day to these powerful mindset exercises, your child can build a solid foundation for mental strength and resilience. These exercises will not only improve their performance on the field but also prepare them for the challenges and opportunities life presents. Remember, with consistent practice and your support, your young athlete can unlock their full potential and develop the mindset of a champion.

As we conclude this introduction to Chapter 2, reflect on the journey you are embarking upon with your young athlete. You've explored the profound impact of the subconscious mind, recognizing its power to shape your child's mental resilience. Additionally, you've gained insight into the importance of aligning inner thoughts with desires, reinforcing the foundation of mental toughness.

The path to mental toughness is multifaceted, and challenges may arise along the way. However, remember that every step taken with your child is a step towards their growth, both as athletes and as individuals who understand the profound connection between their thoughts and their achievements.

Chapter 3: "Mastering Mental Visualization Techniques"

Parents, the mental realm often stands as the true battleground where victories and defeats are decided. You understand that fostering mental resilience, confidence, and focus is as vital as honing physical skills. In this chapter, we embark on a journey into the realm of mental visualization techniques—a powerful tool that empowers young athletes to harness the full potential of their minds.

Every parent desires to see their child succeed, not only in sports but also in life. The path to success in sports is a challenging one, marked by triumphs and tribulations, elation and frustration. Young athletes face immense pressure to perform at their best, and their mental fortitude plays a pivotal role in determining outcomes.

This chapter is dedicated to unveiling the art and science of **mastering mental visualization techniques** that will enable your children to navigate this path with confidence, resilience, and grace.

In the following pages, we will delve into a variety of visualization exercises, carefully crafted to suit the needs of young athletes. These exercises are more than mere mental drills; they are keys to unlocking hidden potentials and unleashing the champion within your child. While each exercise is succinct, it packs a punch, delivering immense benefits when practiced consistently.

One of the fundamental principles of visualization is that the mind cannot distinguish between a vividly imagined experience and a real one.
When young athletes immerse themselves in guided visualization, they are essentially prepping their minds for success. They step onto the field, court, or track with a mental blueprint already etched in their consciousness, paving the way for remarkable performances.
Through these exercises, young athletes can envision themselves facing that penalty kick, sinking that game-winning three-pointer, or executing that flawless gymnastic routine. The more vividly they paint these mental pictures, the closer they come to turning them into reality.
But mastering mental visualization isn't solely about replicating moments of glory. It's also about cultivating the resilience to bounce back from failures. Young athletes will face disappointments and setbacks on their journey. These exercises will equip them with the mental fortitude to view these setbacks not as defeats but as stepping stones toward improvement.

The Importance of Visualization in Sports

In competitive sports, where physical prowess and technical skills are prerequisites for success, the power of the mind often takes a back seat. However, mental strength and visualization are integral components of an athlete's toolkit. This chapter delves deep into the theory behind visualization in sports and the profound impact it can have on an athlete's performance, emphasizing the alignment of desires with emotions as a central theme.

Mental rehearsal or Mental Imagery are other names for visualization. It is a cognitive process where individuals create and simulate sensory experiences in their mind's eye. In the context of sports, visualization involves mentally rehearsing and experiencing various aspects of athletic performance, from executing specific skills to achieving desired outcomes. The underlying principle of visualization is rooted in the mind's remarkable ability to bridge the gap between thought and reality. When athletes vividly imagine themselves performing at their best, their brain processes these mental images as if they were actual experiences. This mental conditioning not only fine-tunes their neuromuscular coordination but also influences their emotional state and overall mindset.

To truly grasp the power of visualization, it's essential to understand the intricate connection between the mind and body. Our thoughts, emotions, and physical actions are deeply interlinked. When an athlete visualizes a perfect golf swing, a flawless penalty kick, or a record-breaking sprint, their brain activates the same neural pathways and muscle groups as if they were physically performing those actions.

The mind's role in athletic performance goes beyond the physical aspect. Emotions play a pivotal role in an athlete's ability to excel under pressure. Visualization allows athletes to align their desires with their emotional responses. When athletes vividly picture themselves achieving their goals, they also experience the associated emotions—confidence, determination, and elation. This alignment between desires and emotions can be a potent force that propels athletes toward success.

Visualization has the remarkable ability to challenge and overcome limiting beliefs that can hinder an athlete's progress. Many young athletes grapple with self-doubt and limiting beliefs, such as *"I'm not good enough,"* or *"I can't handle pressure."* These beliefs create mental barriers that can impede performance.

Let's consider the example of Emma Johnson, the talented young gymnast who has the physical skills needed to excel but is plagued by a limiting belief that she will always fall during her balance beam routines when the pressure is on. Through visualization, she can confront this limiting belief head-on. She begins by visualizing herself confidently performing her routines on the beam, nailing every move flawlessly. As she repeats this visualization, her mind starts to replace the belief of failure with one of success.

Gradually, she starts to believe that she can indeed perform well under pressure. In actual competitions, she now approaches the balance beam with a newfound confidence, as her mind has been conditioned to expect success. Visualization has transformed her belief system and, consequently, her performance.

At the same time, fear and anxiety are common challenges in sports, particularly among young athletes. Visualization serves as a potent antidote to these negative emotions.

Consider Ethan Smiths, the 12 years old tennis player who faces intense anxiety before important matches. Through visualization, he can create mental scenarios where he steps onto the court with poise and confidence. He vividly imagines himself serving aces, executing powerful forehands, and staying calm during challenging moments. This mental conditioning helps him gradually override the anxiety response.

Visualization not only allows all of them to confront their fears but also teaches them how to manage their emotions effectively. The player learns to associate the tennis court with positive emotions and self-assuredness. Over time, the fear that once held them back begins to fade, making way for a more composed and fearless athlete.

Every athlete experiences setbacks and failures at some point. Visualization can be a powerful tool for turning these disappointments into opportunities for growth.

Imagine Alex Williams, the 14 years old basketball player who missed a crucial free throw in a championship game. The memory of that missed shot haunts him, leading to performance anxiety during free-throw situations. Through visualization, Alex can revisit that moment and visualize himself confidently sinking that same free throw.

As guys repeatedly visualize success in this scenario, their perception of that past failure begins to shift. They start to see it as a stepping stone rather than a stumbling block. Visualization helps them extract lessons from defeat and use those lessons as motivational fuel for improvement.

In conclusion, visualization is not merely a mental exercise; it's a transformative process that can elevate an athlete's performance to new heights. By understanding the profound connection between the mind and body, athletes can harness the power of visualization to enhance their skills, boost their confidence, and manage their emotions effectively.

Visualization Techniques for young athletes

Visualization is not a mere mental exercise; it is a fundamental tool for enhancing athletic performance. This technique involves creating detailed mental images of desired outcomes, actions, and performances. It's a process where athletes utilize their imagination to rehearse their skills, strategies, and successes. The significance of visualization lies in its capacity to bridge the gap between the mind and body, harmonizing thoughts, emotions, and actions to optimize athletic performance.

At its core, visualization is about mentally experiencing success before it becomes a reality. It's akin to a mental workout that conditions the mind to adapt and respond optimally when faced with actual sporting challenges. The science behind visualization is grounded in the principle that our minds can influence our bodies. When athletes vividly imagine themselves performing at their best, their brain processes this information in a way that can activate muscle groups and neural pathways associated with the intended action. Visualization isn't a passive mental exercise; it's a dynamic force that propels athletes towards greatness, one vivid image at a time.

Real-Life success stories can be a great example. Renowned athletes often attribute their achievements, in part, to the power of visualization.

Take Michael Phelps, the iconic Olympic swimmer with an unprecedented 23 gold medals. Phelps was not solely reliant on his physical abilities; he was also a master of mental preparation. Visualization was a cornerstone of his success. Before each race, Phelps would immerse himself in a mental landscape where he felt the water's resistance, sensed the rhythm of his strokes, and envisioned himself triumphing. This mental rehearsal significantly contributed to his extraordinary career.

In the realm of gymnastics, we encounter Simone Biles, a gymnast celebrated for her extraordinary talents. While her physical prowess is awe-inspiring, her extensive use of visualization sets her apart. Prior to every routine, Simone meticulously visualizes each movement - from her initial leap to her impeccable landings. This mental rehearsal instills unshakable confidence and a mindset of perfection, consistently translating into stellar performances.
The transformative potential of visualization is not limited to seasoned professionals; it extends to young athletes as well.

Meet Alison Smith, the 14 years old aspiring tennis player with dreams of grandeur. Alison created a vision board adorned with images of her tennis idols and snapshots from grand slam tournaments. This vision board became a daily source of inspiration. Alison would mentally transport herself to prestigious tournaments, picturing herself competing against top players and hoisting championship trophies. Visualization became the driving force behind her motivation and determination, propelling her towards becoming a promising junior player on the brink of national-level competition.

Now, let's explore the practical aspects of visualization techniques for young athletes. While the concept remains the same, the application can vary based on age and experience.

Here are some strategies tailored for young athletes that I use with my daughter Megan:

Create a Mental Movie: Encourage your young athletes to create mental movies of a desired performance. This involves imagining themselves in action, from the beginning to the end, with vivid details. Whether it's scoring a goal in soccer or executing a perfect dive, the mental movie helps them rehearse success.

Use All Senses: Your young athletes should engage all their senses in their visualizations. They should not only see themselves succeeding but also feel the sensations associated with it. For instance, a young sprinter should imagine the rush of wind against their skin and the pounding of their heart as they cross the finish line.

Goal-Oriented Visualization: Help your young athletes set specific goals for their visualization sessions. Whether it's improving their shooting accuracy or perfecting their swing in baseball, having clear objectives enhances the effectiveness of visualization.

Consistency is Key: Emphasize the importance of regular practice. Just like physical training, mental training through visualization requires consistency. Your young athletes should incorporate it into their daily routines.

Overcoming Challenges: Teach your young athletes to use visualization as a tool for overcoming challenges and fears. If they're struggling with a particular skill or facing a tough opponent, they can visualize themselves confidently navigating these situations.

Visualizing Mistakes and Recovery: It's essential to help your young athletes understand that visualization isn't just about success; it's also about learning from mistakes. They can visualize making errors and then visualize their recovery and comeback.

Mindset Exercises: Guided Visualization

In the quest to equip your young athletes with the mental fortitude needed to excel in their chosen sports, mastering the art of mental visualization is paramount. Visualization, often termed **"Guided imagery"** or **"Mental rehearsal,"** is a powerful mental tool that has been employed by both amateur and professional athletes to enhance their performance.

In this chapter, we will explore the significance of guided visualization in sports and provide concrete techniques that you parents can teach your young athletes. These exercises will not only aid in boosting performance but also nurture valuable life skills.

Visualization operates on the principle that **the mind and body are intricately connected.**

When athletes vividly imagine themselves successfully executing their sporting skills, it stimulates neural pathways in the brain, mirroring the actual physical practice. Mental imagery reinforces the neural pathways responsible for muscle memory. When young athletes visualize performing a particular move or technique, their brain registers it as a practice session, contributing to muscle development.

By repeatedly envisioning successful performances, athletes become more confident in their abilities, leading to reduced pre-competition jitters.

It allows athletes to set precise and achievable goals. Through visualization, they can see themselves reaching their objectives, making it easier to translate these mental images into reality.

Visualizing the entire sporting experience, from preparation to execution, helps young athletes maintain unwavering focus during their actual performance.

Visualization encourages athletes to anticipate challenges and devise strategies to overcome them. This mental exercise can be applied to various real-life situations, fostering problem-solving skills beyond the field.

Now, let's delve into practical visualization techniques suitable for your young athletes. These exercises are designed to be concise yet impactful, ensuring they can be completed within a few minute. Remember that consistency is key, and you, the parents, should encourage your children to integrate these exercises into their daily routine.

1. Pre-Competition Visualization (1 minute):

Before a game or competition, your young athletes can sit in a quiet space, close their eyes, and mentally rehearse the upcoming event. They should visualize themselves arriving at the venue, engaging in warm-up routines, and, most importantly, executing their skills flawlessly. Encourage them to focus on the sensory aspects – the feel of the ball, the sounds of the crowd, and the exhilaration of victory.

2. Performance Enhancement (1 minute):

During regular training or practice sessions, your young athletes can take a brief break to visualize themselves refining a specific skill. For instance, a soccer player can visualize making precise passes or taking accurate shots on goal. This exercise can be integrated into training sessions to maximize skill development.

3. Stress Reduction Visualization (1 minute):

Stress and anxiety are common in competitive sports. Your young athletes can practice this exercise when they feel overwhelmed. In a calm environment, they should close their eyes and take slow, deep breaths. As they exhale, they can visualize tension leaving their bodies. Inhaling deeply, they can imagine a wave of calmness washing over them, replacing anxiety with confidence.

4. Goal Achievement Visualization (2 minute):

Your young athletes can sit down with a pen and paper, listing their short-term and long-term goals in sports. Then, they can close their eyes and visualize each goal being accomplished. Whether it's scoring a certain number of points or achieving a personal best, the more vividly they can imagine it, the closer they are to making it a reality.

After a game or practice session, encourage your young athletes to reflect on their performance.

They should close their eyes and replay key moments, focusing on both successes and areas for improvement. This reflective practice fosters a growth mindset, where setbacks are seen as opportunities to learn and grow.

To emphasize the effectiveness of guided visualization, let's explore some real-life success stories of young athletes who harnessed this technique to achieve remarkable feats:

Emma's gymnastic triumph: At just 14 years old, Emma Johnson faced intense competition at a regional gymnastic championship in the water. Her coach introduced her to visualization techniques. Emma visualized herself gliding effortlessly through the water, breaking records. During the championship, her focused and confident performance mirrored her mental rehearsals, resulting in multiple gold medals.

Ethan's success in tennis: Ethan Smiths, the young tennis player, had difficulty with backhand hitting. Through visualization exercises, he mentally tried to repeatedly execute precise backhand serves. In a crucial match when faced with this challenge, he executed his shots with confidence and precision, winning the match

Olivia Wilson, the young and promising soccer player, found herself in a challenging situation during a crucial match. Her team was trailing by a goal, and there was mounting pressure from the opponents. As time was ticking away rapidly, Olivia felt the weight of expectations, both from her teammates and the parents cheering from the sidelines.

In those tense moments, Olivia paused for a moment and closed her eyes. It was an instinctive gesture, a conditioned reflex from the countless times she had practiced visualization. In the darkness of her thoughts, she began to vividly visualize a series of positive images and scenarios for success. She saw herself skillfully dribbling past the opponent, delivering a perfect pass, and finally, scoring an extraordinary goal. She imagined the joy and excitement of her teammates, parents, and coaches as they celebrated her success.

As she focused on these mental images, Olivia began to feel a growing sense of confidence within her. The tension transformed into determination, and the fear of failure gradually dissipated. Her mind was fully immersed in the visualization, as if she were experiencing the moment in real-time.

When she opened her eyes again, Olivia was different. She had regained composure and self-belief. She felt ready to face the match with a positive attitude and a focused mindset. Over the course of the remaining minute, her actions on the field began to mirror what she had visualized.

In the end, Olivia not only contributed to the equalizing goal but also scored the decisive goal for her team's victory. Visualization had given her the mental strength to overcome the challenging situation and turn positive mental imagery into reality on the field. It was a tangible example of how the practice of visualization had helped Olivia handle pressure and reach her potential during a crucial match.

These stories exemplify the transformative power of guided visualization in the lives of young athletes. By incorporating these exercises into their daily routines, parents can empower their children to harness the full potential of their minds in pursuit of sporting excellence.

The real-life success stories of Emma, Ethan, and Olivia serve as living proof of the transformative power of visualization. These young athletes are not exceptional solely because of their physical prowess; they stand out because they have harnessed the potential of their minds. Their stories inspire us to believe that with dedication and guided visualization, our children can also achieve remarkable feats in their chosen sports.

Chapter 4: "Goal Mastery: Unlocking Your Full Potential"

Hi Parents! Welcome back again! there exists a powerful force that drives young athletes to strive for greatness—**goals**. These objectives, whether they involve winning championships, setting personal records, or achieving mastery in a specific skill, act as beacons guiding the way to athletic excellence. However, the path to realizing these dreams is rarely straightforward, and this chapter is dedicated to unraveling the art of goal mastery.

In the preceding sections of this chapter, we've explored the significance of goal-setting in a young athlete's journey. We've delved into the intricacies of goal definition, emphasizing the importance of specificity, measurability, attainability, relevance, and time-bound objectives. These insights are fundamental in transforming vague aspirations into tangible targets.

Goal mastery is not merely about setting ambitious aims; it's about crafting a roadmap that paves the way for achievement. Think of it as building a bridge from where you are now to where you want to be in your athletic journey. Along this bridge, there are pillars, each representing a critical aspect of your goals: Specificity, Measurability, Attainability, Relevance, and Time-boundness. These pillars provide the strength and stability needed to navigate the sometimes challenging terrain of competitive sports.

Imagine your young athlete as an archer, aiming for a distant bullseye. Without a clear target and a well-defined trajectory, hitting the mark becomes a matter of luck rather than skill. Goal mastery equips your child with the tools they need to become the sharpshooter in their athletic endeavors.

In the story of Megan, my daughter, we witnessed how the **SMART criteria** —Specific, Measurable, Attainable, Relevant, and Time-bound — transformed her desire to excel in soccer into a concrete plan. It provided clarity, motivation, and a means of measuring progress. By setting SMART goals, Megan's journey was no longer a vague exploration but a focused mission with a defined destination.

As parents, you play an indispensable role in your child's goal mastery journey. You are the architects of their bridge, guiding them toward their dreams while ensuring the structure is strong and resilient. Your involvement is not about imposing goals on your young athlete but about nurturing their aspirations, providing support, and helping them navigate the complexities of goal-setting.

One of the key responsibilities you bear is to facilitate the goal-setting process. Engage your child in conversations about their dreams and aspirations in sports. Encourage them to be specific about what they want to achieve and help them identify the measurable aspects of their goals. Ensure that their objectives are challenging yet attainable and relevant to their passion for their chosen sport.

Lastly, assist them in setting deadlines, adding the crucial element of time-boundness to their goals.

But your role doesn't end with goal definition. You are also the cheerleader on the sidelines, the provider of resources and opportunities, and the emotional anchor during challenging times. Your unwavering support and belief in your child's abilities can make all the difference in their pursuit of athletic excellence.

The power of goal-setting

Goals are not mere aspirations; they are the guiding stars that lead young athletes on their journey to success. The power of goal-setting cannot be underestimated, and in this chapter, we will explore how setting effective goals can propel your young athletes towards unlocking their full potential.

I always tell my daughter Megan: *"Every achievement, no matter how monumental, begins with a simple act:* **setting a goal**".
Goals provide clarity of purpose, direction, and motivation. They serve as the roadmap that young athletes follow as they navigate the complexities of their chosen sport.
Effective goal-setting is both an art and a science. It involves a thoughtful and systematic approach to ensure that the goals set are not only attainable but also inspire growth and excellence.

Many successful athletes attribute their achievements to effective goal-setting. Take Michael Jordan as an example. Jordan set a series of specific, measurable, and time-bound goals throughout his career.
Early in his career, Jordan set a goal to win an NBA championship with the Chicago Bulls. Not only did he achieve

this goal multiple times, but he also set individual scoring records and won five regular-season MVP awards. Each season, he pushed himself to achieve new milestones, setting records and raising the bar for excellence in the sport.

Michael Jordan is a living example of the value of goal-setting due to his unwavering pursuit of perfection. His ability to consistently set and achieve ambitious goals not only made him an iconic athlete but also an inspiration for young athletes worldwide.

In addition to setting clear and measurable goals, it's essential **to emphasize the importance of constantly pushing boundaries**. Encourage your young athletes to set goals that **challenge them to step out of their comfort zones**. Explain to them that real growth and progress occur when they dare to reach for goals that initially seem beyond their grasp.

For example, if your child is a competitive swimmer and has consistently achieved top positions in regional competitions, encourage them to set a goal of qualifying for national championships. This goal might initially feel intimidating, but it will drive them to train harder, improve their technique, and elevate their performance. By continuously striving for more, they expand their horizons and develop the resilience and determination needed to excel in sports and life.

How to write effective goals

Pay attention Parents! Setting goals is akin to charting a course.

Just as a ship needs a destination and a map, young athletes require clear goals to steer them towards success. In this chapter, we delve into the art and science of writing effective goals for your aspiring sports stars. I'll share essential insights and techniques to help you guide your young athletes on their path to greatness.

Before we dive into the details of crafting goals, let's consider why they are indispensable. Goals serve as a blueprint for achievement. They provide direction, motivation, and a sense of purpose for young athletes. Whether it's winning a championship, improving personal records, or mastering specific skills, goals give athletes something to strive for and measure progress against.

As a parent, you play a pivotal role in helping your child define and pursue these goals. I'd like to share a personal anecdote to illustrate the impact of effective goal-setting in my own experience.

When my daughter, Megan, expressed her passion for soccer, I knew it was essential to channel her enthusiasm in a constructive way. We sat down together, and I encouraged her to articulate her aspirations in the sport. Initially, Megan's goals were broad and vague—she wanted to *"become a great soccer player"* and *"win games."* While these aspirations were admirable, they lacked the specificity needed for effective goal-setting.

I guided Megan through the process of refining her goals. We discussed her strengths and areas needing improvement. Megan realized that her dribbling skills and goal-scoring accuracy required more attention. Together, we set specific goals: *"Increase dribbling accuracy to successfully pass five defenders within three months"* and *"Score ten goals in the upcoming season."*

With these concrete objectives in mind, Megan approached her training with renewed determination. She worked tirelessly on her dribbling techniques and spent extra hours perfecting her shooting accuracy. The quantifiable nature of her goals allowed us to track her progress meticulously. It wasn't long before Megan's dribbling accuracy improved, and she achieved her goal of scoring ten goals in the season.

This experience with Megan reinforced my belief in the power of effective goal-setting. It transformed her passion into a purpose-driven journey. It provided her with clarity and motivation, and most importantly, it allowed her to measure her growth. Megan's story is a testament to how writing effective goals can propel young athletes towards excellence.

There exists a real ABCs of Effective Goal-Setting! Now, let's explore the key principles of writing effective goals for your young athletes.

The foundation of effective goal-setting lies in specificity. Goals should be detailed and clear, leaving no room for ambiguity. When setting goals with your child, encourage them to articulate precisely what they want to achieve. Instead of a vague goal like "improve in soccer," consider a specific objective such as *"score ten goals in the next five games"* or *"increase my dribbling accuracy to 90%."*

Goals must be measurable to gauge progress accurately. Include quantifiable elements that allow athletes to track their achievements. While it's important to encourage ambition, goals must remain within reach. Unrealistic goals can lead to frustration. Collaborate with your child to strike a balance between setting challenging targets and ensuring they are attainable. For instance, if your child's goal is to "become the top scorer in the league," help them break it down into smaller, achievable milestones, such as *"score five goals in the next three games."*

Goals should align with your child's overall aspirations and values. Ensure that the goals they set are directly related to their chosen sport and personal growth. If your child dreams of playing at the collegiate level, their goals should reflect the skills and achievements required for that journey.

Effective goals have a timeframe attached. Establish deadlines that create a sense of urgency and prevent procrastination. A goal without a timeline lacks the impetus for action. For example, *"achieve a starting position on the school team within the next season"* provides a clear timeframe and sense of urgency.

Setting goals is just the beginning. The real power lies in the actions taken to achieve those goals. Work with your young athletes to develop action plans, outlining the specific steps, training routines, and strategies required to reach their objectives. Many professional athletes attribute their success to the power of effective goal-setting.

Take famous soccer player Megan Rapinoe, who plays for the U.S. Women's National Team, as an example. Rapinoe's career is a testament to the impact of well-defined goals.

From a young age, Rapinoe set specific goals for her soccer career. She aimed to surpass the achievements of her peers and become a dominant force in women's soccer. Her dedication to perfecting her free-kick accuracy and dribbling skills stemmed from clear, actionable goals. Rapinoe's story serves as inspiration for young soccer players like my daughter Megan, showing that setting and achieving goals can lead to extraordinary success on the field.

Mindset Exercises: Goal Definition

Setting clear and actionable goals can be a game-changer in their athletic journey. However, it's not enough to have vague aspirations; we need to dive deep into the process of goal definition to make those dreams a reality.

Imagine you're planning a road trip with your family. You're excited about the adventure ahead, but you can't start your journey without knowing your destination and charting your route. Goals are the destinations of our life journeys, and goal definition is like creating a detailed roadmap to reach those destinations. For young athletes, this process is equally crucial.

Goal definition is about converting broad dreams into specific, achievable objectives.

It transforms a desire to "become a great athlete" into a concrete plan with milestones. When your child says, "I want to be a star soccer player," it's your role as a parent to help them define what that means. What skills do they need to excel? What accomplishments will make them a star player? These questions guide the process of goal definition.

One effective approach to goal definition is using the **SMART criteria**, which stands for Specific, Measurable, Attainable, Relevant, and Time-bound. Let's break down each component:

Specific: Encourage your young athlete to be precise about their goals. Instead of saying, "I want to improve in soccer," they might state, *"I want to score 15 goals in the upcoming season."* The specificity provides a clear target.

Measurable: Goals must be measurable to track progress accurately. For instance, if your child's goal is to improve their basketball shooting, they can set a measurable goal like, *"Increase my free throw shooting percentage from 70% to 90% in six months."* Measuring progress helps stay on course.

Attainable: Goals should be challenging but achievable. Your role as a parent is to ensure that the goals are within reach and don't set unrealistic expectations. If your child dreams of becoming a professional athlete, help them break it down into attainable milestones, like earning a spot on a college team.

Relevant: The interests and long-term goals of your child should be reflected in their goals. Ensure that the goals resonate with their dreams and values.

Time-bound: Attach a timeframe to the goals to create urgency and prevent procrastination. A goal without a deadline can lack motivation.

For example, *"Improve my 100m sprint time by two seconds within three months"* adds a sense of time pressure.

Let's revisit the story of Megan, my daughter. When we embarked on her goal-setting journey, we applied the SMART criteria to her aspirations. Initially, Megan expressed her desire to become a great soccer player. We used goal definition to refine her ambitions.

Megan's specific goal became: *"Score 15 goals in the upcoming soccer season!"*

This goal was measurable because Megan could easily track her progress by counting her goals throughout the season. It was also attainable because it challenged her while remaining realistic. Megan was already a talented player, and with dedicated training, reaching this milestone was within her capabilities.

Relevance was a key factor in Megan's goal. She was genuinely passionate about soccer, and her goal aligned perfectly with her interests. It was also time-bound since the soccer season had a clear timeframe, giving her a sense of urgency to work toward her goal.

This process of goal definition transformed Megan's vague desire into a clear, actionable plan. It guided her training, motivated her to practice rigorously, and allowed her to measure her progress throughout the season. Megan's commitment paid off when she successfully scored 15 goals, achieving her defined goal and boosting her confidence as a soccer player.

As parents, you can facilitate goal definition exercises for your young athletes.

Here's a simple **few minute exercise** to help them set SMART goals:

Specific: Ask your child to describe their athletic aspirations in detail. What do they want to achieve in their sport? Encourage them to be specific, outlining their goals precisely.

Measurable: Once the goal is stated, help your child identify a way to measure their progress. What can they track to know they're getting closer to their goal?

Attainable: Discuss whether the goal is challenging but realistic. Is it something they can achieve with dedication and effort? If the goal seems too distant, consider breaking it down into smaller, more manageable steps.

Relevant: Ensure that the goal aligns with your child's interests and values. Does it resonate with their passion for their sport?

Time-bound: Add a timeframe to the goal. When do they want to achieve it? Setting a deadline creates a sense of urgency.

By guiding your young athlete through this exercise, you're not only helping them define their goals but also teaching them valuable life skills like planning, commitment, and resilience.

In conclusion, goal mastery is the cornerstone of unlocking your young athlete's full potential. It's a process that involves clarity, commitment, and continuous effort. Through the SMART criteria, we've discovered the art of crafting well-defined goals that serve as guiding lights in the journey toward athletic greatness.

Megan's story illustrates the transformative power of goal mastery. With your guidance, your young athlete can embark on a similar journey of self-discovery, resilience, and achievement. Whether they aim to score goals, break records, or achieve mastery in their sport, the path to greatness begins with setting clear and actionable goals.

Chapter 5: "Champion Mindset: Insights from the Pros"

As we delve into Chapter 5 of our journey towards unlocking the Champion Mindset, we reach a pivotal moment in our exploration of the world of sports psychology. In the previous chapters, we've examined the critical roles parents play in building mental toughness, techniques to strengthen the subconscious mind, the power of visualization, and the art of goal mastery. Now, we're stepping onto the field with the pros themselves, seeking insights from the very athletes who have mastered the art of winning and performing at their peak.

This chapter revolves around the significance of role models in sports and the invaluable lessons young athletes can learn from professionals who have walked the path to greatness. While parents, coaches, and mentors undoubtedly have a profound impact on young athletes, there's something uniquely inspiring about seeing an accomplished athlete in action. These professionals serve as living examples of what's possible with dedication, resilience, and a champion's mindset.

In this chapter, we'll explore how aspiring young athletes can tap into the wisdom of their sporting heroes and use their experiences as a roadmap to success. We'll delve into the various facets of this mentorship, discussing the profound impact it can have on a young athlete's development. Through real-life stories and actionable advice, we'll uncover how young athletes can emulate the practices and perspectives of the pros to elevate their own game.

Our discussion will be guided by the principles of developing mental toughness, managing expectations, and fostering personal growth, which we've been exploring throughout this book. These principles remain the foundation upon which young athletes can build their own champion mindset.
With that said, let's embark on this journey to uncover the insights and inspirations that professional athletes offer. Let's learn from their experiences, dissect their performances, and understand how they harness the champion mindset to conquer their goals. Together, we'll gain a deeper understanding of the crucial role models play in shaping the future of sports excellence.

The importance of Role Models in sports

Hey parents! Did you know that the road to excellence is illuminated by the inspiring figures who have achieved greatness before us?

These role models in sports serve as guiding lights, instilling the values and attributes necessary for success in aspiring young athletes. In this chapter, we explore the profound significance of these sports heroes and their impact on nurturing the champion mindset.

In the realm of athletics, role models come in various forms. They can be legendary athletes whose names are etched in history books, or they may be contemporary stars whose achievements are still unfolding. Regardless of their status, these individuals possess qualities that make them invaluable mentors for young athletes.

One of the primary roles of these mentors is to provide a tangible example of what can be achieved through dedication and hard work. As parents, you may have observed the spark of inspiration in your child's eyes when they witness their favorite athlete breaking records or achieving game-changing feats. This admiration goes beyond hero worship; it's about demonstrating to young athletes what is possible through unwavering commitment to their craft.

Beyond the physical feats they accomplish, professional athletes offer a treasure trove of knowledge and life lessons that extend far beyond the field or court. These individuals have weathered the highs and lows of competition, grappled with injuries and setbacks, and emerged stronger and more resilient. Their stories serve as testaments to the indomitable human spirit's ability to overcome adversity.

Role models in sports are not just sources of inspiration; they are also reservoirs of wisdom and guidance. Here are some key aspects of how these icons can influence young athletes:
Role models set the standard for excellence. When young athletes watch these individuals in action, they witness the embodiment of commitment, discipline, and relentless effort. They learn that achieving greatness requires more than talent; it demands unwavering dedication to continuous improvement.
The journey to success in sports is paved with obstacles and setbacks. Role models teach young athletes the art of resilience and perseverance. They show that failure is not the end but a stepping stone to future triumphs. Understanding that even the best face adversity helps young athletes cope with their challenges.

Professional athletes often excel not only due to their physical prowess but also their mental strength. Role models demonstrate how to stay composed under pressure, manage anxiety, and maintain focus during crucial moments. These lessons are invaluable in sports and life beyond.

Beyond the scoreboards, role models exemplify sportsmanship, fair play, and respect for opponents. They underscore the importance of integrity and character, teaching young athletes that winning with honor is more valuable than any victory.

Role models often emphasize the significance of a well-rounded life. They demonstrate that success in sports should not come at the expense of one's health, education, or personal growth. This holistic approach encourages young athletes to strike a balance between their athletic pursuits and other life aspects.

As parents, you have a unique opportunity to facilitate this learning process. Encourage your young athlete not only to watch games but to study them. Encourage them to dissect the performances of professionals, analyzing their strategies and mental fortitude. What sets these athletes apart? How do they handle pressure?

What mental resilience do they exhibit in crucial moments? Engage your child in thoughtful discussions that help them internalize the champion mindset.

Learning from Professionals

In the world of competitive sports, the journey to success can be long and arduous. Young athletes, driven by their passion and dreams, often find themselves navigating a challenging path filled with obstacles and uncertainties. It's during these times that role models in sports shine as guiding lights, illuminating the way forward and providing young athletes with the inspiration and wisdom they need to unlock their full potential.

Role models are not mere figures on a distant pedestal. They are living, breathing examples of what's possible through dedication, hard work, and an unwavering commitment to one's craft. Their stories of triumph and resilience serve as powerful sources of inspiration for aspiring athletes. By looking up to these sports heroes, young athletes gain access to a wealth of knowledge and experience that can shape their own journeys in profound ways.

Consider the story of Megan, my young and passionate soccer player with dreams of playing at the highest level of the sport. Her role model is none other than Beth Mead, one of the strongest and most influential female soccer players in America's history. Megan's connection with Beth Mead goes beyond admiration; it's a source of motivation and a blueprint for her own soccer journey.

Megan meticulously studies Beth Mead's performances on the field, not only focusing on her goal-scoring prowess but also on her work ethic and leadership qualities. She watches videos of Beth Mead's matches, where she scores incredible goals, demonstrates impeccable ball control, and leads her team with unwavering determination. Megan's bedroom wall is adorned with posters of Beth Mead, serving as a daily reminder of her aspirations.

Megan's story is just one example of the countless young athletes who draw inspiration from their sports heroes. Let's explore a few more real-life stories to highlight the diverse ways in which role models influence and motivate young athletes:

Ethan Smiths, the aspiring tennis star: Ethan, a budding tennis prodigy, idolizes Roger Federer, a legendary tennis champion known for his incredible mental resilience. By closely following Roger Federer's career, Ethan learns valuable lessons about staying composed under pressure. He applies these lessons during crucial matches and finds himself better equipped to handle high-stress situations.

Olivia Wilson, the Soccer Sensation: Olivia is a rising star in youth soccer, and her role model is Abby Wambach, a renowned soccer player celebrated for her work ethic and teamwork. Olivia not only watches Abby Wambach's games but also reads biographies and interviews to gain insights into her journey. She adopts Abby Wambach's commitment to teamwork and becomes a true leader on the field, inspiring her teammates to perform at their best.

Emma Johnson, the track and field champion: Emma dreams of becoming a world-class sprinter like Usain Bolt, an Olympic gold medalist. She diligently studies Usain Bolt's training regimen, nutrition choices, and mental preparation techniques. By emulating these aspects, Emma continuously improves her performance and inches closer to her own athletic goals.

While professional athletes may seem distant, personal connections can bridge the gap between young athletes and their role models. Initiatives such as meet-and-greet sessions, sports camps led by professionals, or mentorship programs offer valuable opportunities for direct interaction. These interactions allow young athletes to see the human side of their role models and develop a deeper connection.

Another powerful exercise for young athletes is the analysis of professionals' performances. This exercise involves in-depth scrutiny of recordings of their role models in action, dissecting not only their physical techniques but also their mental approaches and strategies.

Let's talk about other guys I've met along the way.

Liam Brown, only years old, is a golf prodigy. He aspires to be a top-level golfer like Tiger Woods, a Masters champion. He spends hours studying footage of Tiger Woods's swings, understanding the mechanics and precision behind each shot. By breaking down these aspects, Liam refines his own golfing techniques and enhances his overall performance on the course.

Sophie Miller, 16 years old, is a figure skater. She's role model is Michelle Kwan, a world-renowned figure skater known for her graceful routines. Sophia meticulously analyzes Michelle Kwan's performances, paying close attention to her choreography, expression, and ability to connect with the audience. Sophia incorporates these elements into her routines, elevating her artistic expression and impressing judges with her performances.

In conclusion, role models in sports are not distant figures but mentors, motivators, and sources of invaluable knowledge. Through their journeys, they teach young athletes the importance of dedication, resilience, and the pursuit of excellence. As parents, coaches, and mentors, it is our responsibility to nurture these connections and help young athletes draw meaningful lessons from the champions who have paved the way. By doing so, we empower the next generation of athletes to chase their dreams with unwavering determination and the belief that greatness is within their reach.

In particular, Megan's path demonstrates the transformational effect of sports idols, as she continues to emulate Beth Mead's dedication, leadership, and skill on the soccer field, steadily progressing toward her own athletic goals.

So, whether it's Roger Federer's composure under pressure, Abby Wambach's teamwork and leadership, Usain Bolt's lightning speed, Tiger Woods's precision, or Michelle Kwan's grace and artistry, these champions offer not just inspiration but tangible lessons that can elevate young athletes' performances and character.

In the chapters that follow, we will delve deeper into the strategies and techniques that young athletes can utilize to develop their own champion mindset, all while keeping in mind the invaluable lessons learned from sports icons.

Mindset Exercises: Analyzing the performances of professionals

Before we dive into the exercises, let's take a moment to comprehend why professionals in the sports arena are such potent role models. These athletes have dedicated years, if not decades, of their lives to honing their skills, managing their emotions, and continuously striving for excellence. Their journeys are often filled with triumphs and tribulations, which make them living repositories of wisdom and experience.

The names Serena Williams, LeBron James, or Simone Biles resonate not only with sports enthusiasts but with anyone who appreciates the dedication, grit, and perseverance required to become the best in their field. They embody qualities that transcend the boundaries of sports and offer valuable life lessons.

Now, let's illustrate how you and your young athlete can practically learn from these professionals.

Meet Megan, my beloved daughter and a rising star in the world of soccer. From a young age, Megan has displayed a deep passion for the sport, and she's always looked up to Beth Mead as her ultimate soccer idol.

Beth Mead's journey from a young, aspiring athlete to a professional soccer star has resonated deeply with Megan, igniting her own aspirations.

As Megan's parent and biggest supporter, I've taken on the role of helping her learn valuable lessons from Beth Mead's performances. Here's a glimpse into our journey and the exercises I've been guiding her through.

Performance Analysis: Together, Megan and I sit down to watch recordings of Beth Mead's games. We don't just focus on the goals and assists; we dive into the nuances of the game. I encourage Megan to pay attention to Beth Mead's off-the-ball movements, positioning, and decision-making. We discuss how Megan can apply these lessons to her own matches and raise her level of play.

Interview Analysis: We seek out interviews or documentaries featuring Beth Mead where she candidly discusses her mindset, training routines, and the challenges she faced. These interviews provide valuable insights into the mental aspects of being a professional athlete. Megan gets to hear firsthand how Beth Mead stays motivated even when facing setbacks, and we discuss how Megan can adopt a similar mindset.

Goal Setting: I helped Megan define reasonable short- and long-term objectives for her soccer career. We discuss how Beth Mead likely established her own goals and the dedication it took to achieve them. I emphasize the importance of setting benchmarks and continuously striving for improvement.

Visualization: I introduce Megan to the concept of visualization. Together, we work on exercises where Megan imagines herself performing like Beth Mead on the soccer field. Visualization is a powerful tool for enhancing performance and building confidence, and we practice it regularly.

Journaling: I provide Megan with a journal where she can document her progress, thoughts, and emotions throughout her soccer journey. This journaling practice helps her reflect on her growth and serves as a tangible record of her development, much like what Beth Mead might have done in her career.

Staying Authentic: While Megan learns valuable lessons from Beth Mead, I constantly remind her to stay true to herself. Beth Mead is an inspiration, not a mold to be fitted into. I encourage Megan to embrace her unique qualities and strengths as she navigates her soccer journey.

Through these exercises and our shared passion for soccer, Megan and I have forged a deeper connection. I've witnessed her growth not only as a player but also as an individual who understands the importance of hard work, determination, and resilience—all qualities that Beth Mead embodies.

Chapter 6: Meditation Mastery for Young Athletes

As we embark on this journey into the heart of meditation mastery for young athletes, it's essential to recognize that the path to excellence in sports is not just about physical prowess and technical skills. While these are undeniably vital components, there's a profound dimension that often remains untapped but holds the potential to elevate young athletes to new heights – the power of the mind.

In the previous chapters, we've delved deep into the mental fortitude required for young athletes to succeed. We've explored the role of parents in shaping their children's mental resilience, harnessed the potential of visualization techniques, and uncovered the secrets of effective goal setting. We've drawn inspiration from champion athletes who've paved the way, and we've discussed the significance of relaxation and mindfulness in enhancing performance.

In this chapter, we'll explore the benefits of meditation specifically tailored for young athletes, share real-world examples of its impact, and provide practical guidance on meditation techniques suitable for kids and teens. But before we delve into the *"how"* let's first understand the *"why"*.

Meditation is often associated with achieving a state of inner peace and tranquility. While this is undoubtedly one of its many gifts, its applications in the world of sports extend far beyond mere relaxation. Meditation is a potent tool for honing the athlete's mind, fostering mental resilience, and nurturing the qualities that set champions apart.

For parents of young athletes, it's essential to recognize that sports is not just about winning games or securing scholarships. It's about nurturing well-rounded individuals who can face challenges with grace, persevere in the face of adversity, and develop essential life skills such as focus, discipline, and emotional intelligence.

Meditation serves as the bridge between the physical and mental aspects of sports. It cultivates a champion mindset by enhancing concentration, managing performance anxiety, and fostering the ability to stay **"in the zone."** It equips young athletes with the tools to harness their inner strength, making them less susceptible to distractions and more resilient in the face of setbacks.

Incorporating meditation into a young athlete's routine can lead to tangible improvements in their performance. It has been shown to enhance focus, sharpen decision-making skills, and boost self-confidence. It's no wonder that renowned athletes, both past and present, have turned to meditation as a secret weapon in their arsenal.

To illustrate the tangible impact of meditation on young athletes, let's look at some real-world examples.

Take the case of Aiden Patel, the 16-year-old aspiring tennis player. Despite his undeniable talent and rigorous training regimen, he often found himself overwhelmed by anxiety during crucial matches. This anxiety led to lapses in concentration and costly errors on the court.

At the recommendation of his coach, Aiden began incorporating mindfulness meditation into his daily routine. Through guided meditation exercises, he learned to stay present in the moment, tune out distractions, and manage the pressure of competition. Over time, Aiden's performance on the court transformed. He not only exhibited improved focus but also displayed remarkable composure during high-stakes matches.

Similarly, consider the story of Lily Jones, a 14-year-old swimmer aiming for the Olympics. Lily faced immense pressure from her parents and coaches to excel, which led to crippling anxiety. Meditation became her refuge, allowing her to cultivate a sense of calmness and self-assuredness. With a clear mind and newfound mental resilience, Lily not only improved her race times but also navigated the challenges of competitive swimming with poise.

These are just two examples of countless young athletes who've harnessed the power of meditation to overcome mental barriers and enhance their performance. These stories underscore the transformative potential of meditation for young athletes, making it a valuable practice for any aspiring champion.

In the following sections of this chapter, we'll delve into practical guidance on meditation techniques suitable for kids and teens. These techniques are designed to be accessible, engaging, and tailored to the unique needs of young athletes.

We'll explore guided meditation exercises that can be incorporated into their daily routines, both at home and in their training environments.

But beyond the techniques themselves, it's essential for parents to understand how to introduce meditation to their young athletes effectively. It's about creating an environment that encourages openness to this practice, ensuring that it complements their athletic journey rather than adding unnecessary pressure.

Benefits of Meditation for young athletes

To understand how meditation influences brainwave frequencies and facilitates creative visualization, it's essential to delve into the science behind this practice. The human brain operates at various frequencies, each associated with different states of consciousness and mental activities. Among these frequencies, four primary categories are relevant to our discussion: Beta, Alpha, Theta, and Delta.

Beta (13-40 Hz): This is the dominant brainwave frequency during our waking hours. It's associated with logical thinking, problem-solving, and active concentration. When athletes are practicing drills, analyzing strategies, or engaging in rigorous physical training, they are predominantly in a beta state.

Alpha (7-13 Hz): The alpha brainwave state is associated with relaxation, creativity, and a heightened state of awareness. Athletes often transition into an alpha state during periods of rest or when they are engaged in creative visualization exercises. This state is optimal for accessing the power of the subconscious mind.

Theta (4-7 Hz): Theta brainwaves are associated with deep relaxation, meditation, and, importantly, creative visualization. In the theta state, the mind is highly receptive to suggestions and can vividly imagine scenarios. It's during this state that athletes can engage in creative visualization to improve their skills and performance.

Delta (0.5-4 Hz): Delta brainwaves are associated with deep sleep and unconsciousness. They play a vital role in physical and mental restoration. While not directly involved in creative visualization, the quality of sleep influenced by delta waves can significantly impact an athlete's overall performance and well-being.

Meditation, specifically mindfulness meditation, provides a structured pathway for athletes to transition from the beta state (active thinking) into the alpha and theta states, where creative visualization can flourish.

During the initial stages of meditation, individuals consciously relax their bodies and clear their minds of distracting thoughts. This transition from the active beta state to the relaxed alpha state is where the doorway to creative visualization begins to open. Athletes learn to let go of external pressures, anxieties, and performance-related stressors, allowing them to access their inner mental landscape.

As meditation deepens, practitioners often enter the theta state. In this state, the brain becomes highly receptive to visualizations and affirmations. Athletes can mentally rehearse their desired outcomes, whether it's mastering a new technique, winning a competition, or achieving a personal best. The vividness and realism of these mental rehearsals can be astonishing, as the subconscious mind is particularly active during the theta state.

Creative visualization, a fundamental component of meditation, allows athletes to harness the full potential of their minds. When they immerse themselves in visualizing their desired outcomes, their brains generate neural patterns that mirror those experienced during actual physical practice. This phenomenon, known as *neuroplasticity*, indicates that the brain forms new neural connections and reinforces existing ones based on the mental images and thoughts it experiences.

For athletes, creative visualization serves multiple purposes. By vividly imagining the precise execution of a skill or technique, athletes can reinforce the neural pathways responsible for that action. This mental rehearsal enhances muscle memory and can lead to improved physical performance.

Athletes can use creative visualization to mentally prepare for upcoming competitions. They visualize themselves confidently and successfully navigating the challenges they will face, instilling a sense of self-assuredness and readiness.

Visualizing long-term goals can provide athletes with a clear sense of purpose and motivation. The mental imagery of achieving their objectives serves as a powerful driving force in their training and competition.

Numerous athletes have utilized meditation and creative visualization to achieve remarkable success. One notable example is Michael Phelps, the most decorated Olympian in history. Phelps incorporated visualization into his training routine, mentally rehearsing every aspect of his races, from the dive off the blocks to the final stroke. This meticulous mental preparation played a pivotal role in his unprecedented Olympic achievements.

Similarly, tennis legend Serena Williams has openly discussed her use of visualization techniques to maintain a winning mindset. Williams visualizes herself executing perfect serves and powerful forehands, which she credits for her sustained excellence on the tennis court.

In the world of golf, Tiger Woods is known for his meticulous mental preparation. He employs creative visualization to navigate complex golf courses mentally, visualizing every shot before he takes it. This practice contributes to his legendary composure and ability to perform under intense pressure.

Meditation, particularly through mindfulness techniques, allows athletes to tap into specific brainwave states that are conducive to creative visualization. By transitioning from the active beta state to the relaxed alpha and theta states, athletes can harness the power of their subconscious minds.

Meditation techniques suitable for kids and teens

In the realm of competitive sports, where young athletes often face rigorous training, academic commitments, and the ever-present challenge of balancing their lives, the importance of mental fortitude cannot be overstated. The ability to stay focused, remain resilient in the face of adversity, and manage stress is as vital to success as physical prowess. Meditation, a centuries-old practice, has emerged as a transformative tool for children and teenagers striving for athletic excellence. By cultivating mindfulness and incorporating meditation techniques into their routines, young athletes can unlock their full potential, both on and off the field.

Fundamentally, mindfulness is the discipline of intentionally focusing one's attention on the present moment without passing judgment. It entails impartially observing one's thoughts, feelings, sensations, and environment.

For young athletes, mindfulness can be a game-changer. It fosters self-awareness, emotional regulation, and an enhanced ability to manage stress, ultimately contributing to improved sports performance.

Numerous professional athletes have embraced mindfulness as a crucial component of their training regimen. They serve as inspirational examples for young athletes seeking to harness the power of meditation.

The greatest basketball player of all time, LeBron James, attributes part of his success to mindfulness meditation. He practices mindfulness to stay focused during high-pressure moments, whether it's a crucial free throw or a game-deciding play. By staying present and blocking out distractions, James maintains a calm and composed demeanor on the court.

The Serbian tennis sensation Novak Djokovic incorporates mindfulness into his training routine. He emphasizes the importance of mental conditioning and meditation to maintain his competitive edge. Djokovic's ability to stay in the moment and remain unfazed by external factors contributes to his remarkable tennis career.

Carli Lloyd, the prominent player for the United States women's national soccer team, employs mindfulness techniques to optimize her performance. She credits meditation with helping her stay focused, manage anxiety, and cope with the demands of high-level competition. Lloyd's exceptional composure during penalty kicks in critical matches showcases the effectiveness of her mindfulness practice.
The Seattle Seahawks quarterback Russell Wilson is an advocate for mindfulness and meditation. He practices

visualization and meditation to enhance his mental clarity, enabling him to make split-second decisions on the football field. Wilson's ability to maintain a strong mental game has been pivotal to his success in the NFL.

To introduce children and teenagers to the world of meditation, it's essential to tailor the techniques to their age, developmental stage, and specific needs.

Here are meditation techniques suitable for young athletes that I apply with my daughter Megan.

Mindful Breathing

Mindful breathing is a foundational meditation technique suitable for all ages. Kids can start by taking slow, deep breaths while focusing on the rise and fall of their chests or the sensation of breath entering and leaving their nostrils. For teens, this practice can be extended by counting breaths and aiming for longer, smoother inhalations and exhalations. Mindful breathing promotes relaxation, reduces anxiety, and enhances focus.

Guided Imagery

Younger children often have vivid imaginations, making guided imagery an engaging meditation technique. Narrating a calming story or scenario can encourage relaxation. They can imagine floating on a cloud, exploring a peaceful forest, or diving into the depths of the ocean. Teens can delve into more complex guided imagery by visualizing their goals, aspirations, and successful performances in detail. Guided imagery enhances creativity, visualization skills, and self-confidence.

Body Scan

The body scan approach is methodically concentrating attention on various body areas. Kids can start with their toes and work their way up to their heads, noticing any areas of tension and consciously releasing it. This practice cultivates physical relaxation and body awareness. Teens can use body scanning to manage physical tension resulting from rigorous training, injury recovery, or general stress.

Loving-Kindness Meditation (Metta)

Loving-kindness meditation, also known as Metta meditation, involves sending well-wishes and positive intentions to oneself and others. Kids can begin with simple phrases like, "May I be happy, may I be healthy, may I be safe." They can extend these wishes to friends, family, and even competitors, fostering empathy and compassion. For teens, Metta meditation promotes emotional resilience and enhances their ability to connect with others in a meaningful way.

Breath Awareness Games

For younger children, turning meditation into playful activities can be highly effective. Games like "Balloon Breath" (slowly inflating and deflating an imaginary balloon) or "Birthday Cake Breath" (pretending to blow out candles) can make meditation engaging and enjoyable. These activities not only introduce mindfulness but also make it a fun part of their daily routine.

Mindfulness in Daily Life

Teens can integrate mindfulness into their daily lives by practicing it during routine activities. Encourage them to be fully present when eating, walking, or performing household chores. This allows them to carry the benefits of meditation beyond designated practice sessions and into their everyday experiences.

Incorporating meditation techniques into the lives of young athletes is not only about enhancing their sports performance but also about nurturing their overall well-being. By promoting mindfulness and meditation, we provide kids with vital life skills that go well beyond the confines of athletic fields. They encompass self-awareness, emotional regulation, resilience, and compassion, qualities that shape them into not just accomplished athletes but also well-rounded individuals. As parents, coaches, and mentors, our role is to guide and support young athletes on their journey towards excellence. Meditation offers a holistic approach to their development, addressing both the physical and mental aspects of their athletic endeavors. It equips them with the tools to face challenges with grace, learn from setbacks, and approach success with humility.

The real-life examples of professional athletes who have embraced mindfulness serve as powerful testimonies to the effectiveness of these practices. LeBron James, Novak Djokovic, Carli Lloyd, Russell Wilson, and countless others have harnessed the power of meditation to elevate their performance and maintain a competitive edge.

As we encourage young athletes to embark on their meditation journey, we plant the seeds of mindfulness that can flourish and bear fruit throughout their lives. By cultivating mindfulness from an early age, we empower the next generation of athletes to not only achieve sporting greatness but also navigate the complexities of life with poise and resilience.

Meditation techniques tailored for kids and teens provide a roadmap to unlocking their full potential, enhancing their mental resilience, and enabling them to excel in the world of sports.

Mindset Exercises: Guided Meditation

Dear parents and fellow young athletes, as we delve into the world of meditation mastery, I want to introduce you to a transformative practice that has become an integral part of my daily routine, one that I share with my daughter Megan, who is a budding young athlete.

Guided meditation is not just a tool for relaxation; it's a powerful method to enhance mental toughness, focus, and overall well-being. Join me on this journey as I walk you through a guided meditation exercise that you can incorporate into your daily lives because it can take just a few minute!

Before we begin, it's essential to create an environment conducive to meditation. Try to choose a place that is calm and uninhabited. If lying down is more calming for you, you can also sit in a cozy chair or on a cushioned surface on the floor. Megan and I prefer sitting cross-legged on the floor, as it helps us feel grounded.

Close your eyes if you feel comfortable doing so, and take a few deep breaths to center yourself. Let go of any tension or stress you may be carrying from your day. Imagine it melting away with each exhalation, leaving you feeling lighter and more at ease.

Now, let's begin with a **body scan meditation**!

This practice helps us become more aware of physical sensations and tensions within our bodies.

Start by bringing your attention to your toes. Imagine a warm, soothing light gently moving up from your toes to your ankles, relieving any tension as it goes. Feel the relaxation spread through your calves, knees, and thighs.

As the light moves up to your hips and lower back, release any tightness or discomfort you may be holding in these areas. Imagine the tension dissolving like ice melting in the warmth of the sun.

Continue to let the light move up to your abdomen, chest, and shoulders. Visualize your muscles relaxing and any stress or worries gently flowing away. Allow the light to flow down your arms, all the way to your fingertips, bringing a sense of calm and tranquility.

Finally, bring your awareness to your neck, throat, and head. Release any tension in your neck and let your facial muscles soften. As the warm light reaches the top of your head, you should feel completely relaxed, from head to toe.

Now that you're in a state of deep relaxation, let's focus on your breath. The breath is an excellent anchor for mindfulness. As you breathe in and out, notice how your chest and abdomen gently rise and fall.

 There's no need to control your breath; just observe it as it naturally flows.

Bring your attention back to your breathing if your thoughts stray from it. Imagine each breath as a wave on the shore, rising and falling in a rhythmic pattern. This simple act of observation can help calm the mind and bring you into the present moment.

Now let us discuss using **Visualization to set intentions.** While in this relaxed state, visualize yourself achieving your athletic dreams. Whether it's scoring a winning goal, crossing the finish line first, or mastering a challenging move, see yourself succeeding in vivid detail.

Feel the emotions associated with your *success, joy, pride, accomplishment.*

Let these positive emotions fill your being as you continue to breathe deeply.

Visualize every aspect of your success, from the sights and sounds to the sensations in your body.

Before we conclude our meditation, take a moment to reflect on all the things you're **Grateful** for in your life, both in sports and beyond. Gratitude is a powerful emotion that can shift your focus from what you lack to what you have.

Finally, let's end with some positive affirmations. Repeat these in your mind or out loud:

"I am strong and capable."

"I am focused and determined."

"I am on the path to achieving my dreams."

Slowly start to become aware of your surroundings to return to the present.

When you're ready, open your eyes carefully and wiggle your fingers and toes. Stretch for a little while before returning to your day.

This guided meditation exercise is a valuable tool that Megan and I practice daily to enhance our mental toughness and stay connected to our goals. With regular practice, you can cultivate a resilient mindset that will serve you well both in sports and in life.

I encourage you to make this practice a part of your daily routine, especially during busy and challenging times. It's not about finding hours in your day; even just five minute of guided meditation can make a significant difference in your mental and emotional well-being.

Remember, meditation is not a quick fix, but a lifelong journey towards self-discovery, resilience, and success. Embrace it with an open heart and an open mind, and watch as it transforms your life, just as it has transformed ours.

Wishing you all the best on your journey to meditation mastery and athletic excellence.

With gratitude and encouragement,
Megan and Micheal Alexi

Chapter 7: Performing at Your Peak: Strategies for Success

Welcome to Chapter 7 of "Performing at Your Peak: Strategies for Success."

Throughout this book, we've embarked on a journey to unlock the full potential of young athletes. We've explored the critical role parents play in building mental toughness, strengthening the subconscious mind, mastering mental visualization techniques, and setting effective goals. We've gained insights from professional athletes, delved into the benefits of meditation, and discovered elite training strategies. We've discussed the importance of relaxation and mindfulness and outlined optimal recovery techniques.

In this chapter, we delve into a fundamental aspect of peak performance - **embracing simplicity.** It's a concept that may initially seem counterintuitive in a world where athletes often seek complex solutions to improve their skills. However, as we'll explore, simplicity can be the key to unlocking a young athlete's true potential.

As a parent or mentor, you're invested in your child's success in sports, education, and life. You want them to excel, to reach their goals, and to enjoy the journey along the way.

Throughout this chapter, we'll delve into the **power of simplicity**, even in just a few minute each day, to transform your child's approach to sports and life.

We'll begin by sharing a real-life example of how embracing simplicity transformed the performance of my daughter, Megan, my passionate soccer player. Her journey highlights the allure of complexity and the profound impact that simplifying her approach had on her confidence, performance, and enjoyment of the game.

We'll also draw inspiration from iconic athletes like Michael Jordan and Cristiano Ronaldo, who achieved greatness by mastering the fundamentals and resisting the lure of unnecessary complexity. These athletes serve as powerful role models for young athletes and illustrate the enduring power of simplicity.

Throughout this chapter, we'll explore an exercise that you, as a parent or mentor, can introduce to your young athlete. This exercise, even if done for just five minute each day, can help them embrace simplicity, improve their core skills, gain mental clarity, and enhance their game awareness. It's a practical tool that aligns with the aspirations of parents and the ambitions of young athletes.

The Mental Game of Peak Performance

As we venture into the heart of Chapter 7, it's crucial to understand that achieving peak performance in sports goes beyond physical prowess. The mental game plays an equally significant role in determining an athlete's success.

As a sports executive in the realm of professional soccer, I've had the privilege of witnessing the intricate dance between the physical and mental aspects of peak performance.

In this chapter, we'll explore the psychology behind achieving excellence on the soccer field, drawing from my own experiences and the stories of iconic athletes such as Michael Jordan, Cristiano Ronaldo, and Lionel Messi. We'll delve into the strategies that have propelled them to greatness and how these insights can apply to soccer, a sport where the mind's strength is just as crucial as physical prowess.

First, let's understand what I mean by peak performance. Peak performance is that elusive state where everything seems to click seamlessly. Athletes describe it as being *"in the zone"* or *"in the flow."*

It's that magical moment when time slows down, and every action feels effortless.

Achieving this state is the ultimate goal for young athletes, and mastering the mental game is the key.

To understand the psychology behind peak performance, we must delve into the mind of an athlete. It's a realm where confidence, focus, and resilience reign supreme. The athlete's mindset is a powerful force that can either propel them to greatness or hinder their progress.

In my role, I've had the honor of working with both rising talents and seasoned professionals in the world of soccer. Soccer, often referred to as *"the beautiful game"*, demands not only technical brilliance but also an unshakable mental fortitude. Whether it was guiding young players through the ups and downs of their careers or helping established stars maintain their competitive edge, the mental aspect has always been central to our work.

One particular experience that stands out is when I worked closely with a talented young striker who possessed extraordinary skills but struggled with consistency in front of the goal. We embarked on a mental training journey that involved visualization, positive self-talk, and goal-setting. Over time, this player's mental resilience improved significantly, translating into a prolific scoring record and a newfound confidence on the pitch.

To illustrate the profound impact of mental strategies on peak soccer performance, let's draw inspiration from the journeys of legendary players.

Considered by many to be one of the best soccer players of all time, Cristiano Ronaldo has a strong mental resilience and work ethic have set him apart. His commitment to mastering the mental aspects of the game, from maintaining focus during high-pressure moments to constantly seeking self-improvement, has been instrumental in his success.

Lionel Messi is another soccer legend. Messi's ability to stay composed and creative under pressure is awe-inspiring. His consistent performances in the world's most challenging soccer competitions showcase his mental toughness and adaptability. Messi's journey underscores the importance of embracing the mental side of soccer.

A timeless icon in the sport is Pele. Pele's unwavering self-belief and ability to thrive in high-pressure situations are legendary. His ability to perform at his best in difficult moments exemplifies the mental strength required to excel in soccer.

These soccer legends serve as compelling examples of how mental resilience, relaxation, and simplicity can elevate one's game to unprecedented heights. Their stories offer invaluable lessons for soccer players of all ages and skill levels, emphasizing the profound influence of mental training on soccer performance.

In the pursuit of peak soccer performance, it's important to recognize that complexity isn't always the answer. Often, the simplest approaches yield the most significant results. This principle is echoed in the words of Cristiano Ronaldo, who once said, *"Talent without working hard is nothing."*

Soccer excellence begins with mastering the fundamentals, such as ball control, passing accuracy, and positioning. By simplifying their approach and dedicating themselves to the basics, soccer players can reduce mental clutter, boost their confidence, and elevate their overall performance.

The mental game of peak soccer performance is a captivating journey where champions are forged. Drawing from my experiences as a soccer executive and the wisdom of soccer icons like Cristiano Ronaldo, Lionel Messi, and Pele, we've explored the critical role of mental training in achieving soccer greatness.

As mentors and guides, our role in nurturing these mental skills is paramount.

Together, we can empower the next generation of soccer stars to unlock their full potential, both on the pitch and in life. The pursuit of peak soccer performance is a testament to the resilience of the human spirit, where the power of the mind knows no bounds.

Reducing Pressure in Performances

Let's delve deeper into the theory of pressure management in the context of sports, drawing on the real-life examples and experiences we've explored.

Whether it's the final minute of a championship soccer game or the deciding point in a tennis match, athletes often find themselves under intense scrutiny, both from themselves and from external sources such as fans, coaches, and the media.

The psychological impact of pressure can be profound. It can lead to heightened stress levels, diminished focus, and a decline in physical and mental performance. Athletes may experience nervousness, self-doubt, and anxiety, all of which can hinder their ability to execute their skills effectively. Pressure primarily manifests in the mind, making mental toughness a crucial component of an athlete's toolkit. Athletes must develop the ability to harness their mental resources to overcome the challenges posed by high-pressure situations.

Allow me to transport you to a memorable evening on the soccer field, where the weight of expectations, the deafening cheers of fans, and the scoreboard painted a tense and pressure-filled picture. As a soccer executive, I've been fortunate to witness countless matches, but one particular game stands out for its invaluable lesson in pressure management.

It was a chilly evening, and our team, which had consistently performed at a high level throughout the season, found themselves trailing 2-0 against a fierce rival. The first half had been marred by missed opportunities, defensive lapses, and an opposing goalkeeper who seemed unbeatable. The players' faces reflected a mix of frustration, anxiety, and determination as they entered the locker room during halftime.

Our coach, Gregg Bradley, a seasoned mentor with a knack for understanding the psychology of the game, took center stage. He knew that addressing the pressure mounting on our young athletes was essential to turning the tide. Here's how he managed to motivate our team to lower the pressure and regain their equilibrium, ultimately leading to a remarkable comeback.

Gregg began by acknowledging the frustration and disappointment the players felt. He assured them that these emotions were natural, emphasizing that even the greatest athletes had experienced similar moments.

Rather than dwelling on the two-goal deficit, Gregg encouraged the team to shift their focus to the present moment. He stressed that the next 45 minute were a new opportunity to showcase their skills and character.

The coach reminded the players of their strengths and past successes, reinforcing their belief in their abilities. He cited examples of miraculous comebacks in soccer history, highlighting that it was not an insurmountable challenge. While emphasizing positivity, Gregg also made tactical adjustments, addressing the weaknesses that had been exploited in the first half. He instilled a sense of purpose by outlining a strategy to claw back into the game.

Recognizing the importance of leadership on the field, Gregg called upon the team's captains and senior players to step up. He reminded them of their responsibility to lead by example and inspire their teammates.

As the second half began, it was evident that the team had absorbed their coach's message. They played with renewed determination, their passes crisper, their movements more purposeful. The fans, who had fallen silent during halftime, now roared in support. The pressure that had weighed down our athletes had transformed into a driving force.

In the final minute of the match, our team managed to level the score at 2-2, securing an improbable draw. The sense of relief, pride, and accomplishment in the locker room afterward was palpable. This game became a defining moment in the players' careers, not just because of the result but because they had learned to manage pressure effectively and respond to adversity.

Pressure is an ever-present companion in the world of sports, and even the most celebrated athletes have faced their fair share of setbacks and defeats. Let's draw inspiration from some famous soccer stars and athletes who turned moments of pressure into opportunities for growth.

Despite his extraordinary talent, Lionel Messi faced criticism early in his career for not performing at his best in big matches. Over the years, he transformed himself into a player known for his composure and brilliance on the grandest stages, proving that even the most gifted athletes can learn to manage pressure.

LeBron's journey to NBA championships was filled with heartbreaking losses and the weight of expectations. His resilience and ability to lead under pressure have made him one of the all-time great basketball players.

Serena Williams, despite her success, has faced countless high-pressure situations on the tennis court. Her mental fortitude and determination to learn from losses have been instrumental in her legendary career.

The soccer match I described and the experiences of athletes like Messi, LeBron, and Serena illustrate that pressure is not a foe to be feared but a challenge to be embraced.

As a soccer executive, I've witnessed firsthand how incorporating pressure management into training can yield remarkable results.

Coaches and athletes can implement the following strategies to prepare for high-pressure situations:

Simulated Pressure Drills: During practice sessions, create scenarios that mimic high-pressure game situations. This can help athletes become more comfortable with pressure and learn to perform under stress.

Sports Psychology Support: Seek the expertise of sports psychologists who can work with athletes to develop mental toughness and pressure management skills.

Pre-Game Routines: Encourage athletes to establish pre-game routines that help them stay focused and calm. These routines can include visualization, meditation, and positive affirmations.

Review and Reflection: After high-pressure games or moments, conduct debrief sessions to discuss what went well and areas for improvement. This can help athletes learn from their experiences and refine their pressure management techniques.

Mindset Exercises: Embracing simplicity

Now we delve into a crucial aspect of peak performance –
embracing simplicity. This concept, while seemingly
paradoxical in a world where athletes often seek more complex
solutions to improve, is a cornerstone of success. I've
personally witnessed its profound impact on my daughter
Megan, as a soccer player, and countless other athletes.

In our quest to excel, we often fall into the trap of complexity.
We seek intricate strategies, advanced training methods, and
cutting-edge technology, believing that the more sophisticated
the approach, the better the results. While these advancements
can indeed offer benefits, they can also lead to undue stress
and distraction.

Megan's journey in soccer epitomizes the allure of complexity.
Like many young athletes, she was eager to explore every
possible avenue to improve her skills. She spent hours
analyzing tactical playbooks, scrutinizing her performance
data, and experimenting with various training techniques. Yet,
despite her dedication, there were times when she felt
overwhelmed, stressed, and, ironically, less effective on the
field.

It was during one particularly challenging season that I
introduced Megan to the concept of embracing simplicity. We
embarked on a journey to streamline her approach to soccer,

focusing on fundamental principles that have withstood the test of time.

So, let's go in this Exercise**: the power of fundamentals (Even in 5 Minute)**

Core Skills: We started by revisiting the core skills of soccer – passing, dribbling, shooting, and defending. Megan spent dedicated practice sessions perfecting these fundamental skills, even if it was just for a brief five minute each day.

Mental Clarity: I encouraged Megan to simplify her mindset. Instead of overthinking every move, she learned to trust her instincts and muscle memory, which she could reinforce in those short daily sessions of around 5 minute.

Game Awareness: We emphasized game awareness – understanding the flow of a match, anticipating plays, and making effective decisions. Megan began to see the game differently, with a newfound clarity, even during those quick practice moments.

Embracing simplicity had a transformative impact on Megan's performance. She felt less pressure to constantly adopt the latest trends in training and tactics. Instead, she channeled her energy into mastering the basics, even if it was just for a few minute each day.

Here's what we observed: Megan's confidence soared as she became more adept at the fundamental aspects of soccer, thanks to those short, focused sessions. She knew that she could rely on her skills in any situation.

The burden of trying to implement complex strategies vanished. She felt liberated from the need to constantly adapt to new and intricate techniques, and those quick practice moments were a respite from the pressure.

Megan's performances on the field became more consistent. She was no longer distracted by overthinking, allowing her to react quickly and effectively, which she honed in her brief daily exercises.

Perhaps most importantly, Megan's enjoyment of the game grew. Soccer became less of a stressful challenge and more of a fulfilling passion, even in those short five-minute practice sessions.

Megan's journey into simplicity aligns with the experiences of many professional athletes who have navigated the complex world of sports.

Consider the legendary Michael Jordan. His game was defined by its simplicity. He mastered the basics – shooting, dribbling, and defense – to perfection. He didn't rely on complex strategies; he relied on his skills, decision-making, and a relentless work ethic.

Another example is Cristiano Ronaldo, one of the most celebrated soccer players globally. His success is rooted in simplicity. He's known for his incredible work rate, relentless practice, and a focus on core skills like shooting and heading. He doesn't chase the latest trends; he excels in the fundamentals, even if it's just for a few minute a day.

As parents and mentors to young athletes, we can impart the invaluable lesson of embracing simplicity, even if it's just for a few minute each day. It's not about discarding advanced techniques or technology; it's about recognizing that true excellence often emerges from mastering the basics.

By helping our children develop a strong foundation in core skills, mental clarity, and game awareness, we equip them to navigate the complexities of sports with confidence and grace. In a world where complexity can breed confusion and anxiety, simplicity offers clarity and serenity, even in those brief practice moments. It's a timeless principle that has the power to transform not only our approach to sports but also our lives.

Megan and many others have learned, sometimes, the path to greatness lies in embracing the beautiful simplicity of the fundamentals, even if it's just for a short while each day.

Chapter 8: "Relaxation and Mindfulness for Enhanced Performance"

Throughout this chapter, we've embarked on a journey to unveil the transformative potential of relaxation and mindfulness techniques for young athletes. Drawing from real-life experiences, practical exercises, and the wisdom of experts, we've explored how these tools can elevate your child's athletic performance.

As we delve deeper into the significance of relaxation in training and the art of practicing with calmness, we invite you to envision a world where your young athlete not only thrives on the field but also possesses the inner strength to conquer the challenges of life beyond sports. This chapter serves as a bridge, connecting the physical and mental realms of athletic excellence, paving the way for holistic growth.

In our exploration, we've uncovered the pivotal role of relaxation in the training regimen of young athletes. It extends beyond the concept of post-training recovery; relaxation becomes a cornerstone of mental resilience and overall performance. We introduced the concept of *"5-Minute Mindful Breathing,"* a brief yet powerful exercise designed to provide immediate stress relief, enhance focus, and foster emotional resilience.

This exercise acts as a testament to the profound impact that even a few minute of mindful relaxation can have on a young athlete's journey.

Within the realm of relaxation, we've delved into techniques for practicing with calmness, drawing inspiration from the **Mindfulness-Based Stress Reduction (MBSR) program** initiated by Jon Kabat-Zinn. By embracing the art of mindfulness, young athletes can develop the ability to live in the present moment, fostering heightened awareness, and promoting mental clarity.

The importance of relaxation in training

In the relentless pursuit of excellence in sports, it's easy to get caught up in the whirlwind of rigorous training regimens, high expectations, and intense competition. Young athletes often find themselves balancing school, sports, and social commitments, with pressure and stress lurking at every corner. This chapter explores a crucial aspect of athletic development - the importance of relaxation in training.

As parents, mentors, and coaches of budding athletes, it's essential to understand that relaxation is not merely lounging on a sofa but a strategic tool that can significantly impact a young athlete's performance, both physically and mentally. In this section, we'll delve into the theory and practice of relaxation techniques and discuss their profound effects on athletic performance and overall well-being.

Relaxation in the context of athletic training doesn't mean slacking off or taking it easy. Instead, it refers to the deliberate practice of calming the body and mind to optimize performance.

One of the fundamental principles of relaxation is learning **to live in the present moment**. In a world filled with distractions and pressures, this skill can be transformative for young athletes. Being fully present during training and competitions allows athletes to perform at their best.

Here's how it works: one of the fundamental principles of relaxation is learning to live in the present moment. In a world filled with distractions and pressures, this skill can be transformative for young athletes. Being fully present during training and competitions allows athletes to perform at their best and make well-informed decisions.

Often, athletes may dwell on past mistakes or missed opportunities. This not only saps their confidence but also distracts them from the task at hand. By learning to let go of the past and focusing on the here and now, your young athletes can perform without the burden of past experiences, enabling them to make decisions based on the current situation.

The fear of what might happen in the future can be paralyzing. Young athletes may worry about making errors or failing to meet expectations. Relaxation techniques teach them to quiet these future anxieties, enabling them to concentrate on the immediate moment and the actions required. This allows them to make decisions in real-time without being clouded by future uncertainties.

When athletes live in the present moment, they can channel their physical and mental energy effectively. This heightened state of awareness allows for better decision-making, quicker reflexes, and a stronger connection between mind and body. Athletes can assess the current situation accurately and make decisions that align with their goals.

The practice of living in the present moment, often referred to as mindfulness, has its roots in ancient Eastern philosophies, particularly Buddhism. Mindfulness meditation, as we know it today, evolved from these ancient practices and was introduced to the Western world in the mid-20th century.

Jon Kabat-Zinn was a major player in introducing mindfulness to the West. At the University of Massachusetts Medical School, Kabat-Zinn established the **Stress Reduction Clinic** in 1979, which is where he created the **Mindfulness-Based Stress Reduction (MBSR)** curriculum.

This program aimed to help individuals manage stress and improve their well-being through mindfulness meditation.

Let's examine two actual instances of young athletes who, with their parents' and mentors' assistance, incorporated relaxation techniques and living in the present into their training routines.

Aiden, the talented young tennis player, used to get overwhelmed by the pressure of important matches. His parents introduced him to mindfulness meditation, emphasizing the importance of focusing on the present moment during rallies. Aiden learned to stay calm and concentrated on each stroke, rather than worrying about winning or losing. This newfound mental clarity not only improved his game but also his overall well-being.

Emma, the dedicated gymnast, often struggled with fear and anxiety when attempting challenging routines. Her coach introduced her to relaxation exercises that helped her stay present during her routines. Emma learned to trust her training and focus on executing one move at a time. This approach not only reduced her anxiety but also led to remarkable improvements in her performance.

By sharing these stories, we highlight the practical application of relaxation techniques and living in the present in the lives of young athletes. It's a testament to the effectiveness of these practices in enhancing their skills, managing emotions, and achieving success.

In conclusion, the importance of relaxation in training, combined with the ability to live in the present moment, cannot be overstated. By incorporating mindfulness and relaxation into the training routines, you empower children to perform at their best, manage stress, and enjoy the journey of athletic development.

Techniques for Practicing with Calmness

As a seasoned sports executive, I've had the privilege of witnessing firsthand the transformative power of relaxation techniques within the realm of competitive sports. These techniques are instrumental in fostering a sense of calmness that can profoundly impact the performance and well-being of young athletes. In this chapter, I'll share some of the invaluable techniques I've encountered over the course of my career.

The Mindfulness-Based Stress Reduction (MBSR) program has been a game-changer in helping athletes of all ages manage stress and anxiety effectively.

These techniques aren't just limited to athletes but can be embraced by you parents as well, creating a harmonious and supportive environment for your young athletes!

During my tenure as a sports executive, I had the privilege of working closely with a group of young athletes who were part of a pilot program aimed at integrating mindfulness into their training routines. The results were nothing short of remarkable. These athletes not only excelled in their respective sports but also exhibited a level of mental resilience and emotional intelligence that set them apart.

One of the key principles of mindfulness is **consistency**. Like any other skill, mindfulness techniques require regular practice to yield significant results. As parents and mentors, it's crucial to encourage your young athletes to incorporate these practices into their daily routines, even during non-competitive periods. Consistency will enable them to reap the full benefits of mindfulness, from improved performance to enhanced well-being.

A very effective mindfulness technique is centered around the breath. It's a practice that can be incorporated seamlessly into a young athlete's daily routine, offering both immediate and long-term benefits.

The 4-7-8 Breathing Technique

A particularly valuable technique for calming the mind is the 4-7-8 breathing exercise. It's simple, can be done anywhere, and yields remarkable results when practiced consistently. Here's how it works. You parents can sit together with your young athlete children and practice the relaxation technique together.

Locate a Quiet Area: To start, look for a place to sit or lie down that is calm and cozy. It's best to practice this technique without distractions.

Close Your Eyes: Gently close your eyes to eliminate visual distractions. This allows you to turn your focus inward.

Relax Your Body: Take a moment to scan your body for any tension. Consciously release any tightness in your muscles, starting from your toes and moving up to your head.

Inhale for 4 Seconds: Take a quiet, slow, four-count mental breath via your nose. As you do this, focus your attention solely on the act of breathing. Feel the air entering your nostrils and filling your lungs.

Hold for 7 Seconds: After your 4-second inhale, pause and hold your breath for seven counts.During this pause, maintain a sense of calm and stillness.

Exhale for 8 Seconds: Now take a gentle, full, eight-count breath out through your mouth. As you exhale, imagine releasing any stress or tension with your breath.

Repeat the Cycle: This completes one cycle. Begin again by inhaling for four seconds, holding for seven, and exhaling for eight. Continue this cycle for several minute.

The 4-7-8 breathing technique induces a sense of calmness by slowing down the heart rate and calming the nervous system. Young athletes benefit from it since it helps them focus their minds on the here and now and let go of worries and distractions.

As you practice this technique regularly, you'll notice that the mind becomes increasingly calm and centered. Athletes who incorporate this practice into their routines often report a sense of mental clarity and heightened focus.

Initially, you might find it challenging to maintain the specified breath counts. It's perfectly normal for the mind to wander or for the breath to feel uneven. With consistent practice, however, you'll gradually improve.

Begin with a few minute of practice each day, preferably in the morning or before bedtime. As you become more comfortable with the technique, you can gradually extend the duration to 10, 15, or even 20 minute!

The ideal outcome is a state of calmness where your mind naturally operates at a lower frequency of mental chatter. Athletes who have mastered this technique often report moments of profound mental stillness, which can be invaluable during high-pressure situations.

Incorporate this practice into your young athlete's routine, and encourage them to use it not only for performance enhancement but also as a tool for managing everyday stress and anxiety. With dedication and consistency, the power of focused breathing can help your child achieve a calm and resilient mind.

In the following sections, we'll explore additional relaxation exercises and mindfulness practices that can further enhance both performance and well-being.

Mindset Exercises: Relaxation Exercises in 5 Minute

Relaxation exercises are a cornerstone of enhanced athletic performance, offering young athletes powerful tools to reach their peak potential. These exercises extend beyond post-training recovery; they serve as potent means to fortify mental resilience and overall athletic prowess.

To underscore the potency of relaxation exercises, let me recount a real-life scenario involving my daughter, Megan, and her soccer teammate, Allison.

As a parent deeply committed to Megan's sporting journey, I understood how important mental and emotional health are to athletic performance. Consequently, I introduced a brief yet highly effective relaxation exercise into Megan and Allison's routine, under the guidance of their soccer coach.

The Exercise: 5-Minute Mindful Breathing

One of the simplest and most effective relaxation techniques we incorporated was 5-Minute Mindful Breathing. This exercise is designed to promote immediate relaxation, making it ideal for young athletes who need a quick mental reset. Here's how we introduced it:

Setting Aside Time: We designated a mere 5 minute after each soccer training session for this exercise. This brevity ensured that it seamlessly fit into their busy schedules.

Comfortable Position: Megan and Allison would find a quiet spot within the soccer facility, sit or lie down comfortably, and close their eyes. The emphasis was on creating a serene environment conducive to relaxation.

Focused Breathing: They were instructed to shift their attention to their breath. The idea was to just watch the breath as it naturally happened, without trying to manipulate it.

Inhalation and Exhalation: The young athletes concentrated on how their bodies felt as air entered and exited them. They counted each inhale and exhale, aiming to reach a count of ten breath cycles.

Acceptance of Distractions: If thoughts or distractions arose during the exercise, Megan and Allison were encouraged to acknowledge them without judgment and then gently redirect their focus to the breath.

After 5 minute, the exercise concluded. Megan and Allison slowly opened their eyes and transitioned back to their regular activities.

The impact of this brief but potent relaxation exercise was remarkable.

Here are some of the benefits Megan and Allison experienced:

5-Minute Mindful Breathing offered rapid stress relief. After intense training sessions or challenging academic days, it provided a quick mental reset, leaving them feeling calmer and more composed. The exercise improved their ability to concentrate during training sessions and matches. They could effectively set aside distractions and maintain unwavering focus on their performance.

Megan and Allison developed greater emotional resilience. They learned to navigate the highs and lows of competitive sports with composure, reducing the impact of performance-related stress. Achieving a calm state of mind through mindful breathing also enhanced their decision-making abilities during high-pressure situations on the field.

The brevity of the exercise allowed Megan and Allison to practice it regularly. They utilized 5-Minute Mindful Breathing not only after training sessions but also before important matches and even during breaks between classes when academic stress loomed.

As parents, encourage your child to incorporate 5-Minute Mindful Breathing into their routine, especially during moments of heightened stress or when they need to regain focus quickly. Its brevity makes it accessible, and its impact can be transformative.

Chapter 9: Young Athletes' Elite Training Methods

Parents, welcome to Chapter 9 of "Elite Training Strategies for Young Athletes." In the following pages, you'll discover the essence of the *Warrior Mentality*—a mindset that encompasses unshakable determination, mental toughness, resilience, positive self-belief, and adaptability. You'll witness how these attributes can transform young athletes into champions. We'll also share personal anecdotes and success stories, including one from the legendary Michael Jordan, to illustrate the real-world impact of this mentality. Moreover, we'll provide practical exercises and strategies that parents and coaches can implement to nurture the Warrior Mentality in their young athletes. These exercises will help athletes stay focused under pressure, bounce back from failures, and maintain a positive self-image.

Warrior Mentality is not just about winning in sports; it's about instilling qualities that empower young athletes to overcome obstacles, adapt to change, and emerge as resilient individuals who approach challenges as opportunities for growth.

Strategies for intensive training

Elite training is more than just pushing the physical limits; it's about optimizing every aspect of an athlete's potential. It's a rigorous and comprehensive approach, aiming to refine skills, enhance performance, and develop mental resilience. While the path to elite training varies depending on the sport, the principles remain consistent.

The journey toward elite status begins with a commitment to mastery. Young athletes need to embrace the idea of continuously improving their skills. They must embrace obstacles and see failures as opportunities for improvement, embracing a growth mentality. For every successful athlete, there are countless hours of dedicated practice behind the scenes.

Each athlete is unique, and elite training recognizes this fact. A cookie-cutter approach doesn't suffice when striving for greatness. Coaches and trainers tailor training programs to the individual athlete, considering their strengths, weaknesses, and developmental areas. This personalized approach maximizes growth potential.

Elite training is built upon incremental progression. It's a gradual climb up the ladder of excellence, with each step forward reinforcing the athlete's confidence and competence.

Celebrating small victories along the way helps maintain motivation and passion for the sport.

Visualization is a powerful tool used by elite athletes to mentally prepare for competitions. Young athletes can benefit from incorporating visualization techniques into their training routines. By vividly imagining themselves performing at their best, they become more confident and focused when the actual moment arrives.

Elite athletes understand that their bodies are their most valuable assets. Nutrition plays a pivotal role in maintaining peak physical condition. Young athletes need to be educated about the importance of a balanced diet and proper hydration. Conditioning programs tailored to their specific sport help build endurance, strength, and agility.

Elite training strategies are not just the domain of athletes; they require collaboration among athletes, coaches, and parents. The commitment to mastery, individualized training, incremental progression, visualization, and proper nutrition and conditioning collectively contribute to transforming young athletes into elite competitors.

You, parents, play an essential role in providing the necessary resources, including financial support, and emotional encouragement. You offer a stable foundation, allowing young athletes to focus on their training and development.

In the pursuit of elite training strategies for young athletes, real-life cases exemplify the application of these principles. Below, we delve into various scenarios that showcase the strategies used by young athletes in their journey toward excellence.

Alex's Basketball Ascent

Alex Williams, a 15-year-old basketball player, had his sights set on becoming an elite athlete. His journey began with a commitment to mastery. Alex recognized that success in basketball required more than just natural talent; it demanded relentless practice and skill refinement.

Alex dedicated hours each day to perfecting his dribbling, shooting, and defensive maneuvers. He worked closely with a personal coach who designed drills tailored to his specific needs, helping him build a strong foundation of basketball skills.

Understanding that every player is unique, Alex's coach devised a training program that capitalized on his strengths and addressed his weaknesses. This personalized approach accelerated his development and allowed him to excel in areas where he previously struggled.

Alex's journey was characterized by continuous improvement. He celebrated small victories along the way, such as achieving a higher shooting accuracy or successfully executing a challenging play. These achievements fueled his motivation and propelled him toward his goal.

Emma's Journey in Gymnastics

Emma Johnson embodied the essence of elite training strategies in her pursuit of excellence.

She recognized the importance of mental strength in gymnastics. She incorporated positive affirmations into her daily routine, repeating phrases like *"I am strong and confident"* to boost her self-belief.

Emma's parents played a vital role in her journey. They ensured she followed a balanced diet rich in nutrients essential for her physical demands. Her conditioning program was customized to enhance her strength, flexibility, and endurance – all crucial for gymnastics.

Emma's coaches emphasized the importance of incremental progression. She practiced routines and individual elements repeatedly, making slight improvements with each session. This approach instilled a strong work ethic and resilience in her.

Noah's Ascent in Swimming

Noah Anderson, the 14-year-old competitive swimmer, embarked on a path to excellence in the pool. Noah harnessed the power of mental imagery. Before major swim meets, he would vividly imagine himself gliding through the water with impeccable form and precision. This mental rehearsal helped him enter races with unwavering focus and confidence.

Noah's swim coach recognized that each swimmer had unique strengths and weaknesses. Noah received personalized training that addressed his specific areas of improvement, such as refining his technique for the butterfly stroke.

His commitment to mastery was evident in his dedication to early morning and late-night training sessions. He understood that excellence required going above and beyond the ordinary, and his relentless pursuit of improvement set him apart.

Sophia's Journey in Track and Field

Sophia Miller, a 16-year-old track and field athlete, exemplified the principles of elite training in her pursuit of success.

Sophia used goal setting as a key motivator. She would set specific, measurable, and achievable goals for each track event, constantly challenging herself to surpass her previous records.

Sophia's training regimen included a strong focus on nutrition and conditioning. n order to maximize performance, her coach stressed the significance of providing her body with the proper nutrition. Conditioning programs were tailored to improve her speed, strength, and agility.

Sophia's commitment to incremental progression was unwavering. She believed that consistent, small improvements were the building blocks of excellence. This mindset kept her focused on the journey of constant growth.

These real-life scenarios illustrate how young athletes, with the support of dedicated coaches and parents, have successfully implemented elite training strategies. Their commitment to mastery, individualized training, incremental progression, and the power of positive affirmations, mental imagery, and goal setting have propelled them toward excellence in their respective sports.

As we conclude this chapter, it's essential to recognize that elite training is not a one-size-fits-all approach. It requires tailoring strategies to the unique needs and goals of each athlete. By understanding and applying these principles, young athletes can navigate their journey toward becoming elite competitors.

How to tackle challenges

In the journey of young athletes striving for excellence, challenges are an inevitable part of the terrain. These challenges come in various forms, from physical obstacles to mental hurdles, but it's in facing and overcoming them that athletes truly grow and excel. We will explore not only the theory behind tackling challenges but also practical strategies employed by athletes, including my own daughter Megan, to conquer these obstacles.

Before delving into the real-life examples and strategies, it's crucial to understand the theoretical underpinning of tackling challenges in sports. Challenges, whether in training or competition, are not roadblocks; they are opportunities for growth.

Confronting challenges often demands the acquisition of new skills or the refinement of existing ones. When young athletes face challenges head-on, they have the chance to enhance their abilities.

Overcoming challenges builds mental toughness and resilience. Athletes learn to bounce back from setbacks, which is a valuable life skill.

Successfully tackling challenges boosts an athlete's self-confidence. It serves as a reminder that they can overcome obstacles, fostering a positive mindset.

Challenges can force athletes to adapt to changing circumstances, a skill that proves invaluable in sports and beyond.

Now, let's explore how these theoretical concepts manifest in real-life scenarios.

Megan, my daughter, plays soccer with a passion that matches her dedication. Recently, she faced a significant challenge during a crucial match against a top-tier opponent. Megan's team had been performing exceptionally well throughout the season, but this particular game was proving to be their toughest test yet.

The opposing team was known for its defensive prowess. Megan's team had struggled against them in the past, often finding it challenging to break through their solid defense. As a midfielder, Megan's role was pivotal in creating scoring opportunities, but she knew that her team needed to find a way past the formidable opponent's defense.

Megan's coach, Steve, recognized the challenge and adjusted the team's tactics. They worked on quick passes, coordinated movements, and exploiting spaces in the opponent's defense during practice sessions.

Steve emphasized the importance of mental toughness. He encouraged the team to stay focused, maintain a positive attitude, and not get discouraged by the opponent's reputation.

Megan and her teammates understood that overcoming such a challenge required a collective effort. They communicated effectively on the field, providing support and encouragement to one another.

During the match, Megan and her team applied the strategies they had practiced. They remained patient, passed the ball efficiently, and looked for opportunities to exploit weaknesses in the opponent's defense. Megan's adaptability and mental toughness were on full display as she navigated the challenges presented by the opposing team's defense.

In the end, Megan's team emerged victorious, winning by a narrow margin. It was a hard-fought victory, but it was also a testament to their ability to tackle challenges head-on. The experience not only enhanced Megan's soccer skills but also instilled in her a sense of accomplishment and confidence that extended beyond the field.

Megan's soccer challenge serves as a prime example of how young athletes can overcome formidable obstacles. By embracing challenges as opportunities for growth, adapting to changing circumstances, maintaining mental toughness, and relying on teamwork, they can conquer even the most daunting opponents.

To further illustrate the power of overcoming challenges, let's look at the incredible journey of tennis legend Serena Williams.

Throughout her career, Serena Williams, one of the best tennis players of all time, had several difficulties.

Perhaps one of the most daunting was her battle with health issues. In 2011, she suffered a pulmonary embolism, a life-threatening condition. She not only had to overcome this health scare but also faced career setbacks due to injuries.

For her recovery, she applied the steps of a real strategy.

Resilience: Serena's resilience shone through during these challenging times. She underwent rigorous rehabilitation and training to regain her strength and form.

Positive Mindset: Serena maintained an unwavering belief in her abilities. She refused to let setbacks define her and instead focused on her goals.

Adaptation: Serena adapted her playing style to accommodate her physical condition and age, proving that adaptability is key to longevity in sports.

Serena Williams not only returned to professional tennis but also continued to dominate the sport.Following her health scare and hardships, she won multiple Grand Slam titles, solidifying her place among the best athletes in tennis history.

Serena Williams' inspirational journey highlights the transformative power of tackling challenges head-on. By embracing challenges as opportunities for growth, adapting to changing circumstances, maintaining mental toughness, and relying on teamwork, young athletes can conquer even the most daunting opponents.

As parents and coaches, it's essential that we instill in our young athletes the belief that challenges are not barriers to success but stepping stones toward it. When they approach challenges with this mindset, they are not only more likely to excel in sports but also better equipped to navigate the challenges life throws their way.

We'll delve into the idea of mental toughness in more detail in the next section "Warrior Mentality," a strong frame of mind that equips young athletes to succeed in the face of difficulty.

Mindset Exercises: Warrior Mentality

In the competitive arena of youth sports, developing a warrior mentality is paramount for young athletes aiming to excel. This mindset goes beyond physical prowess and delves into the realm of mental toughness, resilience, and unwavering determination. As a parent and a coach, I have witnessed the transformative power of instilling a warrior mentality in young athletes, including my daughter Megan.

Now, we will explore mindset exercises that nurture this powerful approach to sports and life.

Personally, I use the specific **Warrior Strategy that** I learned during my *"Unleash Your Mental Strength"* training course.

At its core, the warrior mentality embodies several key attributes:

Unshakable Determination: Warriors approach their goals with an unwavering resolve. They are not easily deterred by obstacles or setbacks but instead view them as challenges to conquer.

Mental Toughness: This mindset cultivates mental fortitude, enabling athletes to maintain composure and concentration under pressure. When it counts most, it helps them perform at their peak.

Resilience: Warriors bounce back from failures and defeats with renewed vigor. They see failures as chances for development and education.

 Self-Belief: Self-confidence is the foundation of the warrior mentality. Athletes with this mindset believe in their abilities and maintain a positive self-image.

Adaptability: Warriors are flexible and adaptable. They embrace change and adjust their strategies as needed to achieve their objectives.

Let me share a personal anecdote about my daughter Megan. Megan's journey to embrace the warrior mentality began during a pivotal moment in her soccer career. Megan's team had encountered a challenging phase marked by a series of losses. They were struggling to find their rhythm, and morale was dwindling. As a midfielder, Megan felt the weight of her team's expectations to create scoring opportunities and maintain possession of the ball.

As Megan's coach and parent, I introduced her to a powerful mindset exercise called **"The Warrior's Pledge."** This exercise aimed to instill the attributes of a warrior mentality into Megan's approach to soccer.

Determination: Megan committed to giving her best effort in every practice and game, regardless of the team's recent performance. She embraced the idea that every match was a chance to improve.

Mental Toughness: We practiced visualization techniques of 5 minute a day to help Megan stay focused and composed under pressure. She learned to visualize successful plays and maintained a positive mindset.

Resilience: Megan was encouraged to view losses as opportunities for growth. After each defeat, we discussed the lessons learned and how to apply them in future games.

Positive Self-Belief: I emphasized the importance of self-confidence. Megan recited affirmations daily to reinforce her belief in her abilities and her role on the team.

Adaptability: We worked on adjusting her playing style based on the team's needs and the opponent's strategies. Megan learned to be flexible in her approach while staying true to her strengths.

Over time, Megan's dedication to the Warrior's Pledge began to yield remarkable results. Her determination translated into improved performance on the field. She displayed mental toughness during critical moments in matches, making key plays and scoring crucial goals. Losses no longer demoralized her; instead, they fueled her desire to grow as a player.

As Megan and her teammates embraced the warrior mentality collectively, their team dynamic transformed. They went from a losing streak to a winning streak, with Megan's leadership and newfound mindset playing a pivotal role.

To further illustrate the impact of the warrior mentality, let's look at the legendary Michael Jordan. His relentless determination and unyielding mindset made him one of the greatest basketball players in history.

Michael Jordan faced his fair share of challenges, including being cut from his high school basketball team. Despite the setbacks, he never wavered in his belief that he could achieve greatness in the sport.

When he used the Warrior Mentality?

Unshakable Determination: Jordan's determination to prove himself drove him to work tirelessly on his skills. He was known for his relentless practice regimen.

Mental Toughness: In crucial moments, Jordan's mental toughness shone. He was unfazed by pressure, often making game-winning shots in high-stakes situations.

Resilience: Setbacks only fueled Jordan's desire to succeed. He used failures as motivation to improve and push himself to new heights.

Positive Self-Belief: Jordan had an unshakable belief in his abilities. He knew he was the best and played with unwavering confidence.

Adaptability: Jordan adapted his playing style as he aged, relying more on his basketball IQ and leadership qualities to continue dominating the game.

For a year Micheal Jordan trained alone, by following the Warrior Mentality Strategy. At 19 years old he led North Carolina to the college title with a shot with a few seconds left in the final. He was Olympic champion at 21 years old. Michael Jordan's warrior mentality not only led him to multiple NBA championships and accolades but also inspired countless athletes worldwide. His experience is proof of this mindset's transformational potential.

In conclusion, the Warrior Mentality is a game-changer for young athletes striving for excellence. By instilling determination, mental toughness, resilience, positive self-belief, and adaptability, we empower them to conquer challenges not only in sports but also in life. Megan's journey and the legacy of athletes like Michael Jordan serve as inspiring examples of the profound impact of this mindset. As parents and coaches, let's nurture and celebrate the warriors within our young athletes, pointing them in the direction of prosperity and development as individuals.

Chapter 10: Optimal Recovery and Mental Performance

I sit down to write this chapter and my mind drifts back to countless evenings spent on the soccer field, watching my daughter Megan pour her heart and soul into her training. The sunsets, the cheers of teammates, and the camaraderie all served as the backdrop to her incredible journey in sports. It's in these moments of reflection that the importance of optimal recovery and mental performance truly comes to life.

Throughout this book, we've explored the multifaceted world of sports parenting and young athlete development. We've delved into the depths of mental toughness, visualized success, and honed the skills required for peak performance. Now, we embark on a new chapter—one that's equally pivotal to Megan's soccer journey and the journeys of countless young athletes out there: Optimal Recovery and Mental Performance. The concept of recovery isn't confined to physical recuperation alone; it extends far beyond that. It's about the restoration of a young athlete's body, mind, and spirit after the rigors of intense training and competition. It's the bridge that connects one practice session to the next, one game to the following, and one season to the next.

Recovery after training

As I stood on the edge of the soccer field, the sun setting in the horizon, I couldn't help but reflect on the intense training session my daughter Megan had just completed. The practice had been grueling, pushing her both mentally and physically. Watching her and her teammates give their all, I knew that recovery was as crucial as the training itself.

This chapter will discuss how important it is to recover from training, its impact on young athletes, and strategies to ensure optimal recovery.

Recovery is the unsung hero of athletic performance. It's the phase where the body heals, adapts, and grows stronger. For young athletes like Megan, who train rigorously to reach their peak potential, understanding the significance of recovery is paramount. So, what makes recovery so essential?

Physical Restoration: After intense training, the body experiences muscle fatigue, micro-tears in muscle fibers, and depletion of energy stores. Recovery allows these physical aspects to repair and regenerate. Without adequate recovery, young athletes are more prone to injuries, fatigue, and a decline in performance.

Mental Rejuvenation: Just as physical fatigue sets in, mental fatigue can also take its toll on young athletes. The demands of training, competitions, and balancing other aspects of life can be mentally draining. Recovery provides a mental break, helping athletes regain focus, motivation, and mental clarity.

Growth and Development: For adolescents like Megan, who are still growing, recovery plays a vital role in growth and development. It's during rest that the body releases growth hormones, repairing and strengthening bones, muscles, and other tissues.

Recovery is a holistic process that encompasses physical, mental, and emotional aspects. By understanding its importance and implementing effective recovery strategies, parents can support their young athletes on their journey towards excellence.

Now, I'll tell you about my specific experience.

Mental cooldown techniques

When the evening sky turned pink and orange as the sun went down below the horizon, I found myself sitting in the quiet corner of our family room, a place that had witnessed countless discussions about sports, dreams, and life. My daughter, Megan, had just finished an intense training session, leaving her physically exhausted and mentally drained. It was during these precious moments of tranquility that I introduced Megan to the concept of mental cooldown techniques – a practice that had played a significant role in my own athletic journey and had the potential to reshape hers.

Recovery isn't limited to physical aspects alone. The mental strain and fatigue young athletes endure during training sessions and competitions can be equally, if not more, taxing. This is where mental cooldown techniques come into play. They serve as a bridge between the physical and mental realms, allowing athletes to not only recuperate physically but also find solace and rejuvenation for their minds.

Megan, like many young athletes, had often struggled with maintaining a healthy mental state after demanding training sessions. The intensity of sports can sometimes lead to stress, frustration, and anxiety. Without proper mental cooldown techniques, these emotions can linger, affecting an athlete's overall well-being and future performance. As a parent deeply invested in Megan's athletic journey, I felt compelled to introduce her to these valuable tools that could safeguard her mental health and, in turn, enhance her performance.

Over the years, I had experimented with various mental cooldown techniques, and I was excited to share them with Megan.

As we settled into our cozy corner, I began by explaining the significance of <u>controlled breathing</u>. Deep, intentional breaths, I told her, could work wonders in calming the mind. We practiced diaphragmatic breathing together, inhaling slowly through the nose, allowing the abdomen to rise, and exhaling through pursed lips, releasing any tension that had built up during training.

Next, I introduced Megan to the power of <u>mindfulness meditation</u>. We started with a simple guided session. I encouraged her to close her eyes, focus on her breath, and let go of any intrusive thoughts. This practice not only helped her relax but also enabled her to gain a better understanding of her own thoughts and emotions.

<u>Visualization</u> was another crucial aspect of our mental cooldown routine. I shared stories of renowned athletes who used visualization to enhance their performance. Megan and I practiced visualizing her future successes – the feeling of crossing the finish line, the sound of the crowd cheering her

name, and the overwhelming sense of accomplishment. This exercise not only motivated her but also provided a positive mental image to carry forward.

Incorporating <u>Gratitude</u> into our mental cooldown routine was essential as well. I encouraged Megan to reflect on her training session and identify the aspects she was grateful for – the support of her coaches, the camaraderie with her teammates, and the opportunity to pursue her passion. Expressing gratitude helped shift her focus from any perceived shortcomings to the abundance of positive elements in her sports journey.

As Megan and I continued to practice these mental cooldown techniques, I witnessed a remarkable transformation in her approach to sports. She became more resilient in the face of challenges, her ability to manage stress improved, and her self-belief grew stronger. Beyond the physical gains of training, Megan was evolving into a mentally tough athlete, equipped with the tools to navigate the intricate landscape of competitive sports.

Our mental cooldown sessions also strengthened our parent-child bond. <u>They provided a platform for open communication</u>, allowing Megan to share her fears, frustrations, and aspirations. As a parent, being there to listen and guide her through these moments was immensely rewarding.

These techniques serve as a sanctuary for young minds to find solace, regain focus, and prepare for the challenges that lie ahead. Megan's journey through sports had been transformed, and she was not only growing as an athlete but also as a person.

The mental cooldown techniques we had embraced became an invaluable asset, one that Megan would carry with her as she pursued her dreams, navigated life's obstacles, and emerged as a resilient, mentally tough individual.

In the coming chapters, we will delve further into the strategies and techniques that can empower both parents and young athletes on their quest for excellence in sports and personal growth. Together, we will explore the intricacies of a pre competition day, uncover the secrets of maintaining optimal mental performance, and celebrate the achievements of athletes who have harnessed the power of a balanced mindset.

A comprehensive guide for Pre-competition Routines.

When the sun begins its ascent on the day of a big competition, anticipation and excitement fill the air. The journey that Megan and I have embarked on, one filled with dedication and resilience, has led us to this pivotal moment. The hours leading up to a competition are critical. They set the stage for what's to come and can significantly impact an athlete's mindset and physical readiness.

In our quest for excellence, we've honed a pre-competition routine that is both strategic and adaptable, catering to Megan's specific needs as a soccer player.

Morning Routine - Rise and Shine for Success

6:45 AM - Wake Up and Visualize Success:
Start the day early, encouraging your young athlete to wake up and spend a few moments visualizing their goals. Visualization is a powerful tool to boost confidence and motivation.

7:00 AM - Healthy Breakfast:
A nutritious breakfast fuels their day. Incorporate complex carbs, proteins, and fresh fruits to provide sustained energy.

7:30 AM - Morning Meditation:

Begin with a 5 minute meditation session to promote mental clarity and focus. Guided meditation techniques are particularly effective for young athletes.

Mid-Morning - School and Mental Prep

8:00 AM - School Time:
Prioritize their education. Ensure they're focused and ready to learn, maintaining a balance between academics and sports.
11:00 AM - Positive Affirmations:
Encourage your young athlete to recite positive affirmations. These affirmations boost confidence and create a champion's mindset. It is very helpful to devote yourself to positive affirmations in mid-morning

Lunch Break - Nourish and Recharge

12:30 PM - Nutrient-Packed Lunch:
Lunch should include lean proteins, vegetables, and whole grains. Keep them hydrated with plenty of water.
1:00 PM - Journaling Time:
Have your young athlete maintain a journal to record their thoughts, experiences, and insights from the day.

Afternoon - Training and Skill Development

3:00 PM - Physical Training:
Engage in sport-specific training and skill development. Ensure they follow their training plan, focusing on technique and improvement.

5:00 PM - Goal-Setting Session:
Sit down with your athlete to revisit and refine their goals. Help them set SMART (Specific, Measurable, Achievable, Relevant, Time-bound) goals for their sport and life.

Evening - Recovery and Family Time

7:00 PM - Dinner:
Another balanced meal is essential to support their recovery and growth. Include lean proteins, veggies, and healthy fats.

8:00 PM - Family Bonding:
Spend quality time as a family. This strengthens your connection and provides emotional support.

8:30 PM - Wind-Down Meditation:
A short meditation session before bed helps in relaxation and prepares them for a restful sleep.

Night - Rest and Reflection

9.00 PM - Bedtime Routine:
Ensure they get enough sleep for recovery and growth. A consistent sleep schedule is crucial.

9:30 PM - Gratitude Practice:
Before bedtime, encourage your athlete to reflect on their day and express gratitude for their experiences and learnings.

This daily routine integrates the principles of balancing academics and sports, nurturing mental toughness, and maintaining physical well-being. It's a roadmap to help your young athlete thrive and become tomorrow's champions.

Remember, consistency is key, and with your unwavering support, they'll reach new heights.

Let's empower our young athletes, one day at a time!

Congratulations! you have come to the end of this journey with us.

Use this QRCode to get your Free Bonuses!

Final words for parents and young athletes

Parents and Future Sports Stars,

As we approach the final leg of this empowering journey, it's time to chart the course for the next steps you'll take in your quest for sports excellence. You've absorbed valuable insights, strategies, and guidance throughout this book, and now it's time to translate knowledge into action.

For Parents, it's essential to continue nurturing open communication with your young athlete. Encourage them to share their thoughts, feelings, and concerns regarding their sports journey. Be their pillar of support and trust.

Maintain a balanced approach. Remember the importance of balance in your child's life. It's crucial not to overload their schedules with sports commitments. Ensure they have time for academics, social activities, and relaxation.

If you encounter challenges or issues in your child's sports journey, don't hesitate to seek the assistance of sports psychologists, coaches, or mentors. They can provide valuable insights and strategies to address specific concerns.

Acknowledge and celebrate your child's progress and personal growth, regardless of the outcomes. This helps build their confidence and resilience.

Continue emphasizing the significance of education alongside sports. Explore scholarship opportunities and programs that can assist in your child's academic journey.

Stay updated on the latest developments in sports science, psychology, and nutrition. Knowledge is power, and your understanding can benefit your young athlete.

Teach your child the importance of adaptability in sports and life. They should be prepared to adjust their goals and strategies as they grow and evolve.

For Young Athletes, staying committed is key. Commit to your sports journey with dedication and determination. Consistency and hard work are your allies in achieving excellence.

Continuously refine and set clear, achievable goals. Your goals should challenge you while also motivating you to strive for greatness.

Develop and maintain your mental toughness. Remember the visualization, meditation, and relaxation techniques you've learned. They are your tools for success. Understand that challenges are opportunities in disguise. Learn from failures, and use them as stepping stones toward improvement.

Don't be afraid to seek guidance from your parents, coaches, or sports psychologists when faced with mental hurdles, performance anxiety, or other issues.

Maintain a balanced lifestyle. Make sure you're getting enough sleep, relaxation, and the right kind of food to maintain your physical and mental health.

Continue drawing inspiration from professional athletes and their journeys. Analyze their performances, and extract valuable lessons that can enhance your own.

Consider giving back to your community by sharing your experiences and knowledge with younger athletes. Mentorship is a powerful way to contribute to the sports world.

For Both, support each other. Parents, be unwavering in your support for your young athlete. Athletes, express your gratitude and appreciation for your parents' commitment and sacrifices. Celebrate milestones and achievements together, both big and small. These moments of recognition can strengthen your bond and motivate further progress.

Keep the flame of passion for sports burning. Remember that sports are not just about winning but about personal growth, resilience, and the joy of the journey.

Keep an eye on the long-term goals while appreciating the present. Your collective efforts will pave the way for a bright future.

Micheal Alexi

References and Further Resources

In my quest for excellence in sports, personal growth, and mindful living, I've discovered a wealth of knowledge that has enriched my journey. I wholeheartedly recommend exploring these resources to gain deeper insights and inspiration:

- **Mindfulness and Mental Well-being:**

"The Miracle of Mindfulness: An Introduction to the Practice of Meditation" - Thich Nhat Hanh: Discover the transformative power of mindfulness and meditation, as it has profoundly impacted my own life.
"The Power of Now: A Guide to Spiritual Enlightenment" - Eckhart Tolle: Dive into the world of living in the present moment, drawing from Tolle's wisdom that has guided me in embracing mindfulness.

- **Personal Growth and Inner Strength:**

"Grit: The Power of Passion and Perseverance" - Angela Duckworth: examine the idea of grit and how it can help you achieve long-term objectives; I've found it to be quite helpful.
"Mindset: The New Psychology of Success" - Carol S. Dweck: Unlock the secrets of the growth mindset and how it can empower you to tackle challenges and achieve greatness.

- **Sport and Athletic Performance**

"The Inner Game of Tennis: The Classic Guide to the Mental Side of Peak Performance" - W. Timothy Gallwey: Examine the psychological aspects of athletics, which I've applied to soccer and countless other athletic pursuits.

"Peak: Secrets from the New Science of Expertise" - Anders Ericsson & Robert Pool: Learn the science behind deliberate practice and how it can elevate your performance in sports and beyond.

"The Soccer Handbook: An In-Depth Guide to the World's Most Popular Sport" by various authors: For soccer enthusiasts, this comprehensive guide offers insights, tactics, and strategies specific to the beautiful game.

- **Goal Setting and Achievement:**

"Smarter Faster Better: The Secrets of Being Productive in Life and Business" - Charles Duhigg: Learn how to be productive and effective goal setting, as these principles are transferable to sports and everyday life.

"The 4 Disciplines of Execution: Achieving Your Wildly Important Goals" - Chris McChesney, Sean Covey, and Stephen R. Covey: Discover strategies for turning your sports-related dreams into concrete, achievable objectives.

- **Sport Management and Coaching**

"The Score Takes Care of Itself: My Philosophy of Leadership" - Bill Walsh: Gain leadership insights that transcend sports and can be applied to coaching and managing teams in any discipline.

"Leading with the Heart: Coach K's Successful Strategies for Basketball, Business, and Life" - Mike Krzyzewski and Donald T. Phillips: Learn from the legendary Coach K about leadership, teamwork, and the pursuit of excellence.

It's essential to note that much of what you'll find in these resources is rooted in real-life experiences. My own journey, combined with interactions with parents and young athletes during my personal growth and inner development courses, has provided a profound understanding of the challenges and triumphs that individuals face. These books aren't just theories; they represent lived experiences and lessons that can guide you toward success in sports and life.

I wholeheartedly encourage you to explore these references and further resources, for they have the potential to transform your perspective, fuel your aspirations, and ignite the fire within you to excel, both on and off the field.

Made in the USA
Las Vegas, NV
25 March 2024